The Novels of Hermann Broch

European University Papers

Europäische Hochschulschriften
Publications Universitaires Européennes

Series I

German Language and Literature

Reihe I   Série I

Deutsche Literatur und Germanistik
Langue et littérature allemandes

Vol./Bd. 177

PETER LANG
Bern · Frankfurt am Main · Las Vegas

Malcolm R. Simpson

The Novels of Hermann Broch

PETER LANG
Bern · Frankfurt am Main · Las Vegas

© Verlag Peter Lang, Bern 1977
Nachfolger des Verlages
der Herbert Lang & Cie AG, Bern

ISBN 3-261-02144-6

Auflage 700 Ex.

Druck: Lang Druck AG, Liebefeld/Bern

DEDICATION

To my mother and brother
and in memory of my father.

ACKNOWLEDGEMENTS

The author wishes to acknowledge with deep gratitude the help and encouragement given by Dr. M. Groben, formerly of Tulane University, without which this work would never have been completed, Dr. R. Tinsley of the University of Arizona for his invaluable advice and help, Dr. E.A. Albrecht and all the staff of the German Dept. of Tulane University 1961-1963.

TABLE OF CONTENTS

The biographical sketch, with which I propose to preface this work, is delibe-
rately brief, for two reasons. The main reason is that I propose to concentrate on
the novels themselves, with a view to elucidating some of the obscurities contained
therein and expounding the consistent scheme of ideas that underlies them, in the
hope that the present small circle of Broch's admirers might be substantially expanded. Secondly, this brevity is to some extent dictated by the paucity of material
available.

In a letter to a young person writing a dissertation Broch wrote, "Etwas teile
ich jedenfalls mit Kafka und Musil: wir haben alle drei keine eigentliche Biographie:
wir haben gelebt und geschrieben, und das ist alles" (1). Both in the works and in
his published correspondence there is remarkably little insight offered into his own
life. There are, it is true, autobiographical elements in the work, but they are very
much in the background. These elements will be considered separately, when I
come to the works themselves. The letters, in fact, give less insight into the life
of the author than those of almost any other writer. What does emerge from the
letters is the impression of an extraordinarily noble human being incapable of re-
fusing help to another human being, whether money to needy refugees or encouragement and advice to young writers, despite the enormous demands on his time and
health made by his own work. The letters also testify to a remarkable, ascetic sub-
ordination of the life to the work; indeed, asceticism is the keynote of this heroic
life. Invariably the subject matter is his work -- new projects, discussions of old
works, exposition of his ideas. Only rarely do the realities of everyday life --
economic worries, political crises etc. -- come into the open. More than in the
case of almost any other author the work is the life, and all is sacrificed to the
work, which is regarded as a mission.

Of the basic external facts we are, however, certain. Broch was born in 1886
in Vienna, the son of an industrialist. Since it was intended that he should take over
his father's factories, he studied textile technology at the Webschule in Vienna and
the Textiltechnikum in Mühlhausen, Elsass. This was followed by apprenticeship
in factories in Germany and Bohemia. At first this appealed to him, as he had
"irgendwo den Ehrgeiz, alles zu vereinigen" (2). This is a typical statement, coming from a man who all his life strove to be an intellectual allrounder, who kept a
foot in all, or very nearly all, camps of knowledge. In 1906 he went to America,
"ebenfalls im Dienste der Baumwolle". In 1908 he entered his father's firm, and
later took over its direction, conscious of his responsability for his family, includ-
ing his parents. In 1909 he married Franziska von Rothermann. He remained at
the head of the firm until 1927.

During this time he was "führendes Mitglied des Oesterreichischen Industriel-
lenverbandes", and as such was concerned with labour problems. In his work for
the state employment bureau he helped to combat unemployment. This social activity and experience leaves its mark both on the man, with his ideas of the social
responsability of art, and the late political and sociological works. Furthermore,
this deeply practical experience of life must have been of inestimable value to

Broch the novelist, who indeed shows in many of his works a deep grasp of social realities almost unique in twentieth century German literature.

Aside from this industrial activity, which he considered an imprisonment, he had been pursuing his mathematical studies, going without proper sleep for years, but was only able to do this fully in 1929, when he had left industry. He studied mathematics at Vienna University under Hans Hahn, philosophy under Moritz Schlick and psychology under Karl Bühler. But prior to this he had been working steadily in the field, convinced that no philosophy was possible in this day and age without a mathematical basis. Soon he grew disillusioned with the prevailing positivism in philosophy. At the same time he became more and more interested in those fields of philosophy -- ethics and metaphysics -- which are nowadays seen as having no objective validity, philosophically speaking, and incapable of mathematical treatment:

> Wenn es nicht zu anmassend ist, hier zum Biographischen abzuschwenken, so wäre zu sagen, dass es diese Erkenntnis war, die mich zur ausserphilosophischen, also rein literarischen Arbeit gedrängt hat, d.h. ein Ausdrucksmittel zu finden, das dem ausser-wissenschaftlichen Weltwissen, das jedem von uns innewohnt und ans Tageslicht drängt, genügen könnte. Es ist dies eine Art Ungeduld .... (3).

This subjective sphere is, however, valid in literature, and so, in 1929, he began "Die Schlafwandler".

In 1935 he moved to Mösern, in the Tirol, and then to Alt-Aussee in Steiermark, to work on the "Bergroman", of which more later. At the time of the occupation of Austria by the Nazis Broch was imprisoned in Alt-Aussee (1938), and only rescued from certain death by the intervention of friends abroad. This period sees the genesis of "Der Tod des Vergil".

He emigrated to the U.S.A., after a brief stay in Great Britain, living in New York, Princeton, New Jersey and New Haven and financially assisted by such organisations as the American Academy of Arts and Letters and the Rockefeller Foundation, and commissioned literary projects such as the essay on Hofmannsthal. Although he enjoyed no real financial security at this time, his greatness as a human being is shown in his tireless efforts to help refugees and friends in Europe in need. In 1950 he was made Professor at Yale University. In 1951 he died in New Haven of a heart attack -- doubtless the result of years of overwork -- and was buried in Killingworth, Connecticut.

I should like to conclude this brief introductory sketch by quoting from the first page of Prof. H. Weigand's introduction to "Die Schuldlosen" in the Rhein-Verlag's edition of the collected works; after all, Prof. Weigand has the advantage over the present author of having been privileged to know Broch personally, and his portrait has all the immediacy of personal contact:

> "In einer Bedürfnislosigkeit, die jedem Anspruch auf die Annehmlichkeiten bürgerlichen Komforts entsagte, lebte der alternde Dichter für sein Werk und für die Menschen, die ihm nahestanden. Seine Hilfsbereitschaft kannte keine Grenzen. Sein Wesen strahlte ein Licht und eine Wärme aus, die unvergesslich sind. Sein Profil, mit der starken Nase und dem glatt zurück-

gestrichenen Haar von glanzvoller Schwärze, gemahnte an das eines Nacht-
raben; vor allem durch das grosse, dunkle Auge von unbeschreiblicher
Klarheit, darin Ernst und Mutwille sich zum Ausdruck altersloser Weisheit
vereinigten" (4).

1. THE EARLY WRITINGS

Broch's first literary efforts appeared in the newspaper "Der Brenner", edited by Ludwig von Ficker, a friend of Georg Trakl. Apart from Trakl, other contributors to the paper numbered amongst their ranks Else Lasker-Schüler, Theodor Däubler, the lyric poet Felix Grafe, and Theodor Haecker. It is surpising to what extent the ideas of the mature Broch are anticipated in these early works, revealing the unity of his life and work. The later Broch is already evident here, to the attentive reader, in these early writings. Broch's development consists, in fact, not in constantly exploring new areas but in deepening and expanding ideas which he held from the start. We find, for example, in the Notizen zu einer systematischen Aesthetik (1912) evidence of his preoccupation with the experience of unio mystica, "das mystische Entzücken des tat twam asi ... . ausgeübt durch die Erkenntnis der Einheit von Denkgesetz und Weltgesetz" (1) -- ideas which were later to assume great importance in the creative work.

The sonnet "Mathematisches Mysterium" from November, 1913, covers similar ground:

Gemessen tut sich Unbewusstes auf
Und im Unendlichen entschwebt die Welt.
Ich fühle, wie sich Urteil fällt;
Erstaunend folg' ich seinem Lauf.

Auf einsamen Begriff gestellt
Ragt ein Gebäude steil hinauf:
Und Fügt sich an den Sternenhauf
Von ferner Göttlichkeit durchhellt.

Gebunden muss das Ich erkennen,
Dass es die Wahrheit in der Form nur hält
Und mag an dieser kalten Flamme wohl verbrennen.

Doch sind der Form Erscheinungen auch ungezählt,
Nichts kann sie von der Einheit trennen.
In tiefster Tief' erscheint: durchsonnt die Welt (2).

Whatever reservations one may have as to the aesthetic merits of this poem, it is of the most profound interest to the student of Broch's works for, as Ernst Schönwiese comments,

"das Erstaunliche an ihm ist, dass es mit wenigen Sätzen sofort die Grundidee formuliert, unter der hinfort Leben und Werk Hermann Brochs stehen werden. Es ist das Wissen um das Mysterium der Erkenntnis, um die Begegnung mit dem Unendlichen hier in dieser endlichen Welt, das Wissen um den geheimnisvollen Augenblick der Einswerdung zwischen dem Unendlichen und Endlichen, der unio mystica, das Wissen um das Irrationale, das über allem Verstande der Verständigen ist, denkerische und dichterische Erkenntnis in einem, ... (3).

At the end of Notizen zu einer systematischen Aesthetik, under the subtitle
Unfähigkeit zum Stil, having shown the interrelatedness of art and ecstasy, Broch
argues that style, being the particular form that art and ecstasy take in a particular
epoch, symbolises the epoch and its culture: "Kultur und Stil sind durchaus einheit-
lich, und wenn Ekstase Einheitlichkeit ist, so mag Stil als die Ekstase einer ganzen
Epoche angesehen werden" (4). The basic idea of art as a barometer of culture, as
it were, is found elsewhere, noteably in the work of Spengler and Sedlmayr, but I
do not feel it apposite to discuss the question of possible influences at this juncture,
indeed the early date of the work (1912) precludes the possibility of Sedlmayr's influence. We are concerned here solely with the genesis of Broch's aesthetic and
cultural-historical ideas.

To continue the argument: the ornament, furthermore, can be seen as the
most refined characteristic of style, an abbreviation of style. Broch sees the lack
of style as the essential characteristic of the present epoch, and therefore concludes that this is symptomatic of a lack of culture. Furthermore, typically, he
sees this as part of an inevitable cultural-historical process:

> Jeder Stil stirbt an diesem allzu grossen Wissen; der leuchtende Ausdruck
> einer Wahrheit wandelt sich zu Hohlheit und wird zu Lüge, stirbt. Dann
> kommt der Totengräber, der Rationalist.
> Jeder müden Kultur ersteht der Rationalist, der den gesunden Menschen-
> verstand auf den alten Stil loslässt: die Griechen hatten ihre Sophisten,
> das Christentum seine Reformatoren, das Ancien Régime seine Aufklärer,
> doch diese Zeit versammelt die ganze Horde.
> Denn diesmal ist es gründlicher. Nicht ein Stil will enden, eine Zivilisation
> schickt sich dazu an (5).

The diagnosis of our times as an epoch of decadence, the cultural-historical view
of this process of cultural decline, the regarding of the arts as a kind of barometer
of society's cultural health -- all these ideas were to find expression in "Die
Schlafwandler", in fact are the main ideas of that work. There is no main idea in
the "Zerfall der Werte", which forms the philosophical core of Broch's first novel,
not already present in the earlier essay. In the intervening years Broch has merely
developed, systematized, deepened, expanded.

In "Philistrosität, Realismus, Idealismus der Kunst", published on the 1st
of February 1913 in the "Brenner", in which Broch defends Thomas Mann against
the charge of being a philistine, made by Carl Dallago in the same magazine, we
find a definition of art, based on Schopenhauer's aesthetics, which the Broch of
the later works could well have written:

> künstlerisches Sehen ist die Fähigkeit, in den Objekten deren "platonische
> Idee", das "Ding an sich", zu ahnen; künstlerisches Schaffen heisst, dieses
> Ahnen im Materialen manifestieren zu können (6).

In a letter to Ludwig von Ficker of 18th May, 1913 we find another of the ideas
which were to dominate the mature Broch's work, from "Die Unbekannte Grösse"
to "Der Versucher" and the late works: the concept of felt, intuitive knowledge.
The following passage, indeed, seems to sum up "Die Unbekannte Grösse":

Mit der Voraussetzung der Intuition haben Sie wahrscheinlich Recht, doch scheint es mir, als dehne sie sich viel weiter -- nämlich auf mein ganzes (auch das sog. verstandesmässige) Denken -- aus. Sehen, Empfinden (und was ist Intuition anderes!) ist Voraussetzung jedes Denkens (wenigstens als vorbildender Impuls) und was ich denke, ist wohl stets primär im Gefühl entstanden. Auch die mathematische Wahrheit ist nicht zu errechnen, sondern muss vorher gefühlt sein (7).

In "Die Strasse", published in "Die Rettung", 20th December, 1918, written in the form of a letter to the editor, Franz Blei, we find passages which anticipate the later writings on mass-psychology and politics. With visionary power and great sociological insight Broch recoils, horrified, from the spectacle of mass behaviour:

Ich bin, wie die meisten Menschen, von Massenpsychosen sehr leicht beeinflussbar. Wenn 3'000 Menschen die Wacht am Rhein singen, würgt es mich ebenso gerührt und erschüttert im Hals, wie wenn sie die Marseillaise sängen. Vielleicht ist es diese lächerliche Hingabe, die bei mir solch starkes Reagieren erfordert (8).

Having defined the essence of a real community as "das gemeinsame metaphysische Wahrheitsgefühl und die Verankerung der letzten Einsicht in einem Glauben", Broch points out that it is precisely this shared feeling of truth, a common set of values, which is lacking in the modern mass. It is a "mass", in fact, rather than a community. As such they can be manipulated by a clever demagogue in any political direction. I need hardly point out how subsequent history has vindicated Broch's theories. Broch goes on to define politics as synonymous with justice -- evidence of the deep belief in democracy which never left him, and which was to find full expression in the political writings of his exile in America. However, in this day and age, pure politics must be directed to the mass of humanity,

sie ist also auf ihre Dogmatisierung innerhalb des Massenaggregates von Mündern, Nasen, Bärten, Bäuchen angewiesen. Es gibt keinen anderen Weg für das Geistige, als den der absoluten Erniedrigung als leeres Massenschlagwort, und je höher und je reiner das sittliche Wollen ist, das sich im Politischen manifestiert, desto tiefer ist sein Sturz und seine Verluderung in der billigen Ekstase der Masse (9).

The end of this essay is full of the cultural pessimism which later found expression in "Die Schlafwandler". Indeed, a passage such as the following could have been taken from the later work:

Damit aber steht man im Mittelpunkt des Grauens. Gleichwie es dieser Zeit vorbehalten war, alle Werte sukzessive erstarren und hypertrophieren zu lassen, so muss in notwendiger und nicht abwendbarer Folge nunmehr die Periode des absolut Politischen, das heisst nichts anderes, als die Periode der dogmatisierten Gerechtigkeit und damit Demokratie kommen. Und dieser Periode ist es vorbehalten, auch den letzten Wert, den der reinen Geistigkeit, auf nichts zu reduzieren. Nur die allerroheste Behauung des Geistigen und des Wortes ist noch möglich, denn es muss auf offener Strasse vom Balkon der Masse zugeschrien werden. Die christliche Gemeinschaft hatte noch zu diesem Zweck die Kirchenpredigt, so dogmatisch auch diese noch sein mag. Die gemeinschaftslose Masse hat nur ein paar in die Strasse gebrüllte Vokabeln, Silben von Vokabeln (10).

Typically, Broch sees as the only antidote "ein Wiedererwachen des Wissens um die Verbundenheit aller Dinge im Metaphysischen" (11).

2. "DIE SCHLAFWANDLER"

Broch's theories of history, and in particular of the cultural decline of the West, as outlined in the "Zerfall der Werte", find creative expression in his first novel, "Die Schlafwandler", published in 1931-2. The "Zerfall", which is now reprinted as a separate essay in the collected works, was originally part of the novel, its separate chapters forming part of the involved, contrapuntal architecture of the third volume. The artistic purpose was to illuminate the various parallel, individual histories, which are so artfully interwoven in the "Huguenau", showing the socio-cultural and metaphysical reasons for the frustrations and tortured aspirations of the individual characters.

The image of life which emerges from "Die Schlafwandler" is a pessimistic one. The action is set against the background of a complete valuative vacuum; the possibilities of salvation reveal themselves to be false. Human communication has broken down, "keiner sieht den Anderen im Dunkel", the only reality the fear of death, the Void, which is the unifying strand running through the various episodes, all variations on the same theme. Writing of "Die Schlafwandler" Broch observes:

> er ist von der Ueberzeugung bedingt, dass das autonome und unantastbare Reservatgebiet des Dichterischen in jener tiefsten irrationalen Schichte, in jener wahrhaft panischen Region des Erlebens gegeben ist, dunkles traum-haftes Geschehen, in dem der Mensch bloss gesteuert von Uraffekten, kind-lichen Haltungen, Erinnerungen, erotischen Wünschen, tierhaft und zeitlos dahintreibt. Denn in diesen Regionen versagt der rationale und wissenschaft-liche Ausdruck, das Wort gilt nicht mehr in seiner Eigenbedeutung, nur mehr mit seinem wechselnden Symbolcharakter, und das Objekt muss in der Spannung zwischen den Worten und Zeilen eingefangen werden. - Unverloren und nicht minder schlafwandlerisch aber wirkt im Traumhaften die Sehnsucht nach Erweckung .... aus dem Schlaf, je nach dem subjektiven Vokabular "Erlösung", "Rettung", "Lebenssinn", "Gnade" genannt. Zeiten starker religiöser Bindung haben die dionysisch-apollinische Polarität durch die Bahnung des Traumhaften in bestimmte Werthaltungen weitgehend gelöst; rückgewendet ergab sich, von diesen Werthaltungen aus, die Konstituierung der Sünde (und der tragischen Konflikte des Menschen) -- der Sünde des Triebhaften und Unerweckten, das nicht zu den Werthaltungen vordringt, und der Sünde des Rationalen, Diabolischen, das die Werthaltungen ablehnt oder sie anders gebildet haben will. Grob gesprochen ist dies der Problem-kreis aller ethischen Konflikte, mit denen Dichtung je sich befasste, die die bisherigen Werthaltungen akzeptierte. Hieraus ergibt sich notwendig das neue Problem: wohin wirkt die Sehnsucht nach Erweckung und Errettung, wenn sie in einer Zeit des Verfalls und der Auflösung der alten Werthaltungen nicht mehr in diese münden kann? Kann aus dem Schlaf und Traum übelsten Alltags ein neues Ethos entstehen (1)?

This is the main theme of the three parts of "Die Schlafwandler" -- "Pasenow oder die Romantik, 1888", "Esch oder die Anarchie, 1903" and "Huguenau oder die Sachlichkeit, 1918". The dates 1888, 1903 and 1918 are of great significance, marking, according to Broch, crisis points in the decline of European values. Each novel is written, with great artistic virtuosity, in the style of the period. In all three the central character sees his system of values threatened by the invasion of reality by the Irrational.

The first novel of the trilogy, "Pasenow oder die Romantik", appears, on a casual reading, a straightforward narrative in the style of nineteenth century realism. As Theodore Ziolkowski, in his short study of Broch, writes: "Pasenow is written in such a subtle parody of late nineteenth-century realism the incautious reader might take the novel to be a period piece from the pen of Theodor Fontane -- a comparison that many contemporary critics made." (2) In fact, Broch had not read Fontane at this time (3). The error, however, pays just tribute to the success with which Broch has brought to life a vanished era.

Joachim von Pasenow is a romantic because he clings to values that virtually everyone else regards as outmoded. The army is for him more than a career, it embodies order, hierarchy, and a system of values -- clear, black-and-white values -- in contrast to the vacillating nature of "life", which is something to be feared, and reserved for civilians, who are to be pitied. The significance of the army for Joachim is symbolised in the uniform. The uniform makes quite clear the distinction between the soldier and the civilian.

After the dissolution of the mediaeval value-system, in which all spheres of activity were penetrated by, and subordinated to a central value, there arose a chaos of contending systems, each sphere of activity having its own value-system, which claims absoluteness. Man must face the icy blast of the Infinite. However much he yearns for the lost mediaeval unity of belief and values, he is faced by a chaos of separate value-systems which have become independent, and his only chance is to submit himself to the single value of his profession, to become a function of this value.

The military value-system, symbolised in the uniform, gives Pasenow a feeling of security, is a refuge from the valuative vacuum, in which modern man wanders like a sleepwalker. This whole process of a secular value-system laying claim to absoluteness is romantic, according to Broch, the essence of romanticism being the elevation of the Earthly to absolute status. The cult of the uniform is the specific form which romanticism takes in this age. The concept of uniform takes posession of a man more strongly than any mere profession, because the man who wears a uniform is highly conscious of having found the right way of living and security in his own life.

The man who wears the uniform for many years finds symbolised in it a better order of things than the civilian who exchanges his day-suit for his evening-suit. It is the true function of the uniform to show and establish order in the world and to sublate the chaotic flux of life. Or so, at any rate, thinks Pasenow. However, the feeling of order is an illusion, since it depends on the elevation of the Earthly to absolute status. The army value-system, embodied in the uniform, supplies for Pasenow a flight from the valuative vacuum and from life, with its uncertainties, but no real release from the basic predicament. Pasenow is afraid of life, and the uniform provides an armour, as it were, against its dangers. It is a second skin which protects him from the world and from his own body, enabling him to forget the underwear underneath and the insecurity of life outside. When he is enclosed in his uniform life itself recedes from him.

Proud in his uniform, he doesn't see the civilians in their, to him, strange garb; he cannot grasp that the humanity which exists in such barbaric dress can have anything in common with humanity such as he experiences it. But civilians swim in the whirling pool of life, and he, cut off from life, is dogmatic and un-realistic in his moral judgements. "Auf Unduldsamkeit und Unverständnis ist die Sicherheit des Lebens gegründet" (4). For Joachim the uniform is almost like the priest's habit, separating him from ordinary humanity, symbolising his special status and demanding ascetic devotion to the ideal. He was always annoyed to find men in the barracks with open uniform. He felt there was something indecent in this, a fact which seemed underlined by the regulation forbidding the visitation of certain night clubs when in uniform. Joachim felt it a breach of regulations that there were married officers. When the married Wachtmeister appeared for the morning service and opened two buttons of his uniform to withdraw his prayer book, revealing his checked shirt, Joachim was momentarily disconcerted, until he had checked that his own uniform was fastened. Joachim is posessed by an almost psychotic fear of life; or to be more exact, what he fears is his own subconscious self: he often thinks it would be a good idea if underclothes were made part of the uniform by the addition of medals and decorations, so that the physical self might be forgotten altogether. The humour here, with its fine irony and delicate satire, is almost alone in German literature for its light touch, its avoidance of typical teutonic overstatement, and is a feature of the first volume of the trilogy, being almost totally absent from the other two.

Joachim is glad that the wearing of the uniform prevents him from visiting dubious night clubs. It is, therefore, with some annoyance that he complies with Pasenow senior's wish to go on their traditional round of the clubs in Berlin. In such a night club he meets Ruzena, who opens the door to the chaotic, "dark" forces of the Unconscious. Pasenow is immediately attracted, but with his emotional lethargy and romanticism makes no attempt at this stage to see her again. Instead, he goes for a walk in a part of town out of bounds for officers in uniform, looking for Ruzena's putative lodgings. It is significant that he should seek her lodgings in such a place, since the feelings he has are very much outside the bounds of his self-enclosed conventionality. In the best tradition of nineteenth century German prose the landscape mirrors the mood of man in the landscape. It was a spring evening, spring, of course, being the season of nature's rebirth, much as the feelings Pasenow has are to lead to a spiritual rebirth, a breaking-out of his dead, self-enclosed conventionality, even as in spring nature breaks out of the cold stillness of winter. Even as Pasenow's feelings are topsy-turvy, so nature seems confused and outside its normal routine. The air of anticipation in the landscape mirrors Pasenow's own anticipation:

es gibt Frühlingsabende, deren Dämmerung viel länger währt, als es astro-nomisch vorgeschrieben ist. Dann senkt sich rauchiger, dünner Nebel über die Stadt und gibt ihr jene etwas gespannte Gedämpftheit des Feierabends, der einem Festtag vorangeht (5).

Just as the mist sinks down over the town, so emotion is gradually clouding Joachim's mind. This dusk lasts so long that the shopkeepers forget to close shop and stand chatting with customers in front of the shop until the local policeman smilingly draws their attention to this infringement of the rules. They too, like Joachim, have transcended their normal routine, under the influence of this strange evening.

Joachim imagines Ruzena in "einer Vorstadtwohnung, vielleicht sogar in jenem Kellerlokal, vor dessen dunklem Eingang Grünzeug und Gemüse zum Verkaufe liegt, während Ruzenas Mutter strickend davor hockt und die dunkle fremde Sprache redet" (6). The word "dunkel", which occurs twice in this passage, stands, as throughout the novel, for the unconscious depths of erotic desire. The phrase "dunkle fremde Sprache" really sums up the appeal Ruzena has for Joachim: she awakens the dark, libidinal forces of the unconscious and also has the fascination of the exotic. But Pasenow is still not sufficiently liberated to surrender to this trend of thought and in an attempt to exorcise this image forces himself to imagine Elisabeth, whom his parents want him to marry, going home to the family estate in Lestow, accompanied by her little dog. Elisabeth he always associates with the background of Lestow -- ordered, conventional, safe, insular and predictable. He sees her as a symbol of purity and moral security. The whole novel is the story of his vacillation between these two women, and his eventual choice of Elisabeth -- of convention rather than freedom and real feeling.

Theodore Ziolkowski talks (7) of Pasenow degrading love to pure eros in his affair with Ruzena, but this puritanical view does not do justice to Broch's intention, in my view, and Felix Stössinger is far nearer the truth when he says: "Auch der erotische Rausch kann ein Wahrheitserlebnis sein, denn alles Echte fährt uns in den Himmel" (8). Stössinger, in my view, correctly sees the relationship with Ruzena as something positive: "Ihr Körpermagma erlöst ihn aus der Starrheit der junkerlich-lutherischen Lebensformen, deren er zum Schutz seiner Persönlichkeit in der Hülle der Offiziersuniform bedarf; in ihren Armen wird er wahrhaft nackt und Mensch, so dass sich jede Rückkehr in das Standesleben nur um den Preis des echten Lebens vollziehen lässt" (9). Ruzena's exotic aura, the fact that she comes from another world, is, in fact, of central importance. "Alles Fremde, das unser verschlossenes und erstarrtes Ich beunruhigt, rüttelt es auf, löst seine Begrenzung, zieht seinen Strom in die Lebensströmung hinüber" (10).

Pasenow then meets Bertrand and has lunch with him at a restaurant which they used to frequent as young cadets. Bertrand's restlessness, adventurous spirit and cynicism disturb him. The fact that he is at all disturbed shows that the defences of his conventionality are crumbling, that Bertrand's words correspond to latent possibilities in Pasenow. As yet, however, the conventional prevails. Subconsciously motivated by a desire to escape this temptation, he visits the Buddensens, to restore his sense of security. However, the insular security of the Buddensens' residence, with its well-kept gardens, burbling fountains, the sounds of piano sonatas wafting across immaculate lawns, its air of self-enclosed harmony and rural serenity, leaves Pasenow cold. He feels that he has become alienated, and considers himself for the first time rootless like Bertrand. He feels the visit is empty and wishes Bertrand were there to shake the Buddensens out of their insularity and conventionality.

Joachim meets Ruzena in the street and arranges to have lunch with her. After lunch they go for a walk to Charlottenburg, by the river Havel. The landscape symbolically underlines the spiritual changes that are taking place in

Pasenow. The landscape is full of expectation. There is a prevailing mood of unity, unity between heaven and earth, between the different elements of the landscape, which seems to promote and give its blessing to the growing oneness of Joachim and Ruzena. The sky was "oftmals durch Regenstriche mit der Erde wie zu innigerer Einheit verbunden" (11). The symbolic role of the landscape is again clear as Pasenow is swept into the main stream of life, as everything is dissolved into Schweben:

> Sanft sank der Regen in den Fluss, rieselte leise in den Blättern der Weiden. Ein Kahn lag halb ertränkt im Uferwasser; unter einem kleinen Holzsteg mündete ein Rinnsal mit rascherem Gefälle in das ruhige Gewässer des Flusses und Joachim fühlte auch sich fortgeschwemmt, als wäre das Sehnen, das ihn erfüllte, ein weiches, lindes Fliessen seines Herzens, ein atmendes Gewässer, bangend danach, im Atem geliebten Mundes aufzugehen und zu vergehen wie in einem See unermesslicher Stille (12).

The whole of nature seems to be dissolving, melting, merging its varying forms in a veil of mist, even as Joachim's stiff coventionality is melting, and reason is clouded by emotion, giving way to a desire for unity with the other:

> Es war, als taute der Sommer, so wurde das Wasser erst lind, rieselte es von den Blättern, Tautropfen die Gräser behangen. Ein sanfter Nebelschleier stand in der Ferne, und wandten sie sich um, so hatte er sich auch hinter ihnen geschlossen, so dass ihr Schreiten wie ein Ruhen war; setzte der Regen stärker ein, suchten sie Schutz bei den Bäumen, unter denen der Boden noch trocken lag, ein Flecken trockenen unerlösten Sommerstaubes, fast armselig in all der Gelöstheit ringsum; .... (13)

This love scene, set against the background of a mysterious unity of man and nature, is one of the most beautiful in the whole of German literature, combining great delicacy and great strength:

> Ruzena zog die Nadeln aus dem Hut, nicht bloss weil der städtische Zwang sie störte, sondern auch um Joachim vor den scharfen Spitzen zu bewahren, nahm den Hut ab und lehnte sich mit dem Rücken an Joachim, als wäre er der schützende Baum. Ihren Kopf hatte sie zurückgebeugt, und senkte er sein Gesicht, so berührten seine Lippen ihre Stirn und die Locken, die schwarz sie rahmten. Er sah nicht die dünnen und ein wenig dummen Querfalten auf der Stirn, vielleicht weil er zu nahe war, um sie zu unterscheiden, vielleicht weil alles Schauen zu Fühlen aufgetaut war. Sie aber fühlte seine Arme um sie geschlungen, seine Hände in den ihren, fühlte sie sich wie im Geäst des Baumes, und sein Atem auf ihrer Stirn war wie das Rieseln des Regens in den Blättern; so unbewegt standen sie, und der graue Himmel wurde so eins mit der Wasserfläche, dass die Weiden der Insel drüben wie in einem grauen See schwebten, aufgehängt oben oder ruhend unten, man wusste es nicht (14).

As they return to Ruzena's appartment, Ruzena shakes her head as Joachim is about to go in with her, but the pain of parting is too great for both of them, and

> wie im Traume schon beide, schlafwandelnd sie hinaufstiegen, die <u>dunkle</u> Treppe, die unter den Füssen knarrte, <u>dunklen</u> Vorraum durchquerten und in

dem Zimmer, das im Schatten früher Regendämmerung lag, hinsanken auf
den rauhen Teppich, der das Bett dunkel bedeckte, den Kuss wieder suchten,
aus dem sie gerissen worden waren, ihre Gesichter feucht von Regen oder
von Tränen, sie wussten es nicht. Ruzena aber machte sich frei, führte seine
Hand zu den Haften, die ihre Taille am Rücken verschlossen und ihre singende
Stimme war dunkel: "Mach auf das", flüsterte Ruzena, riss zugleich an seiner
Krawatte und den Knöpfen seiner Weste (15).

I should point out that the underlinings in the above passage are my own. The
adjective "dunkel" has been used from the first in reference to Ruzena and has the
force and function of a leitmotiv. It suggests both the exotic nature of Ruzena, the
Czech girl, and the dark depths of the unconscious, which the relationship with
Ruzena liberates in Pasenow. With the loss of his uniform, this defensive system
erected to protect him from life, he stands naked, a real human being for the first
time in his life, and the experience is one of liberation. Ruzena's smile liberates
him from his stiff, Prussian conventionality, and as he discards his uniform and
starched shirt he gives himself up to the swirling vortex of emotion, to the soft-
ness of her body, and experiences ecstasy.

At this point another major theme of the trilogy is introduced -- thanatos. For
this ecstasy derives from fear, the fear of death. In the forgetfulness of sexual
union they eliminate death momentarily. In enjoying the "Weichheit des Körpers"
they forget for a moment the skeleton which lies underneath. In the unio mystica of
erotic intoxication they transcend the ego, with its participation in the space-time
world which knows death, and share a moment of timelessness beyond death. But
this experience is akin to drug-taking: it is an escape, a momentary forgetting.
The relationship with Ruzena can only provide temporary spiritual comfort for
Pasenow. With a musician's sense of composition, Broch developes the counter-
theme of thanatos in the next section (Helmuth's death). Thanatos and eros are,
in fact, the major themes of the trilogy. In their search for values the "sleepwalkers" try to sublate death, for the function of all values is to negate death. As
throughout the novel, eros and thanatos are seen as interrelated.

Coming at the time it does, Helmuth's death deeply upsets Joachim. "Wäre
es einige Wochen früher geschehen, Joachim wäre vielleicht nicht erschüttert gewesen" (16). Joachim has broken through the chrysalis of dead conventionality
through his relationship with Ruzena and has become, as it were, a human being,
capable of emotion at a time like this. But even more so is he affected by the
consciousness of death as a metaphysical reality. The presence of death seems to
negate reality to such an extent that Joachim no longer recognises the room which
he has known all his life. Only when he recognises the old, familiar, framed iron
cross does he find his way back to the reality of everyday life. Joachim is so
relieved to regain reality, a sense of security, death having stripped him and
revealed him in his spiritual nakedness. But thanatos is only momentarily put on
one side; Pasenow will spend the rest of his life trying to come to terms with
death. In part III we find Pasenow singing with Esch "Rett', oh rett' mich vor dem
Tod, Herr, Zebaoth" (17). The experience of Helmuth's death obviously leaves a
lasting impression on Pasenow's mind. As he watches the passers-by in the street
he reflects "die aufrechte Haltung all der Menschen hier auf dieser Strasse sei eine
völlig unberechtigte, sei unvereinbar mit ihrem besseren Wissen oder ergäbe sich

aus einer traurigen Unwissenheit, da sich doch alle diese Körper zum Sterben werden hinlegen müssen" (18).

Bertrand pays Pasenow a visit of condolence. He reflects upon the stupidity and out-of-dateness of the conventional code of honour, in whose name Helmuth died. Bertrand's words show to what extent he sees through Pasenow's romanticism. Pasenow seems half convinced by Bertrand's arguments but still vacillates. On the one hand he wishes to free himself of inhibiting convention, but on the other hand he feels the danger that he may become like Bertrand if he liberates himself totally from convention. Despite the relationship with Ruzena, which places him beyond the pail as far as the officer's code is concerned, and which liberates him as a human being, Pasenow still feels a gulf between himself and the reality around him. He feels threatened by the seething mass of human beings around him, the soft, fluid mass of life which refuses to permit itself to be classified and systematised according to some rigid doctrine.

With Pasenow in this frame of mind, it is not surprising that he strongly reacts when he receives a letter from his father, suggesting he give up his army career in order to settle in on the family estate and learn to manage it. Such a move, he feels, would drag him down into the morast of civilian life. This, to Pasenow, would be tantamount to robbing him of his protective distance from life, to exposing him to contact with the workers from Borsig's factory. Bertrand's phrase "Trägheit des Gefühls" springs to mind, but he reflects that he is not a coward, and would cheerfully face an opponent in a duel or fight the French in battle. But the dangers of a civilian life were of a different nature -- strange, dark, and unfathomable. In civilian life there was no order, hierarchy, discipline. When Pasenow passes Borsig's factory in the morning or evening and sees the workmen standing before the factory gate, he sees them as a race apart, as foreign and exotic as the Bohemians. Furthermore, to become part of this sinister civilian net, which lay over Berlin, would make him unworthy of Elisabeth. The one thing which could make him worthy of her is the fact that, through his uniform, he differentiates and distances himself from the filth and chaos of civilian life.

Elisabeth makes quite an impression on Joachim with her carefully chosen outfit, which suits her particularly well. She is, for him, a symbol of purity, and he curses his father for daring to think of degrading such a pure creature by giving her to some mortal man. He reflects upon their future relationship. It will have none of the erotic abandonment of his relationship with Ruzena, but will be serious, almost religious in character, in fact so different that the comparison with Ruzena seems almost blasphemous. It would appear that, far from the Ruzena experience uniting Joachim with the main stream of life, he is anxious to "save" her from the civilian net spanning Berlin. She is, as it were, a piece of that reality which he tries to transform and adapt to his own ideals. This is an attempt doomed to failure, for she finally reverts to her callgirl activities.

The theme of thanatos is now taken up again, undergoing subtle variations and maintaining the musical structure of the whole. Even the Buddensens, with their apparent bourgeois security and settled, secure existence, are not exempt from it. Elisabeth realizes that the passion of her parents for celebrating the most trivial occasion and always surprising each other with presents has a deeper meaning. Their compulsive desire to surround themselves continually with new things is the same drive which impels the collector to strive for a complete collection and thereby attain personal absoluteness and the sublation of death. Broch has some interesting remarks to make on the collector in his essay "Psychologie der 'Pursuit of Happiness' ":

> keiner kann, trotz Hitler, die ganze Welt "haben", auf dass er sich sodann mit ihr identifizieren kann. Oder um bei Hitler zu bleiben: das materielle "Haben" muss zum Vernichten, zum Mitnehmen ins Grab werden. Und wer darauf besteht, mit materiellen Stücken, die er sich aus der Welt zueignet, sein Ich, sein "Ist" aufzubauen, wird zum Geisteskranken oder wenigstens zum Neurotiker, zum Geizhals, zum Sammler, zum Wüstling, zum Lust-mörder (19).

Value, Broch tells us, is the sublation of death, or an elimination of the conscious-ness of death. If death means the extinction of the ego, then every extension of the ego shows that death is being kept at bay, so to speak. A human being lives as long as he is capable of accomplishing extension of the ego, and begins to die as soon as contraction of the ego occurs. Where the collector, rake, miser err is in thinking that an infinite extension of the ego can be attained by means of possessions. Their striving after a totality of values is fruitless, because no-one can posess the whole world. Hence the collector's never-ending, insatiable collecting activity. On the other hand, every piece of the world transformed by the ego can become its real posession, but symbolically.

This Broch calls "die Ich-Erweiterung durch Produktivität, die Ich-Erweite-rung durch den geformten Wert" (20). Man, in this way, posesses the world in cognitive symbols, forms it into knowledge and through knowledge can re-form material reality so that it becomes "culture", timeless as truth, a symbol of his overcoming of death. Culture in its entirety is the symbolic overcoming of death. Both the Buddensens and Joachim are posessed by a dominating fear of death. According to Broch the only antidote is a maximal extension of the ego through values. The Buddensens chose the way of physical extension of the ego by means of material "values". They are collectors, obsessive collectors. Pasenow's way is the second way -- that of "Ich-Erweiterung durch den geformten Wert". How-ever, Joachim makes the mistake of embracing an outmoded value-system, of taking refuge in the ideals of the past, whereas, with evidence of the European cultural decadence all around us, what is needed, as Broch sees it, is a search for new values, a new sublation of death. "Die 'Freiheit', auf die es letzten Endes in allem wahrhaft Ethischen immer ankommt, nimmt auf überkommene Werte keine Rücksicht, ..." (21).

Pasenow senior is also preoccupied with thanatos. The death of his son, Hel-muth, has not only filled him with a personal sense of loss, but has also brought him face to face with death as a metaphysical reality. An "inexplicable and myste-rious reason" draws him toward the pastor, although he does not particularly like the man, a vague hope that this man who preached in the church, whose mission is to give the flock spiritual strength and a belief in life after death, might help him to overcome death in himself and come to terms with it. Pasenow is also afraid of death, and avoids the topic when the pastor mentions Helmuth. At other times he desires its presence, crying "warm" when the pastor speaks of Helmuth, like a child playing the game of hide-and-seek.

As Pasenow grows increasingly confused, the military mystique loses much of its symbolic importance for him. Watching some cadets taking riding instruction he sees the whole thing as a circus. He no longer wears his uniform with the same natural ease, and questions the conventions of the military life, such as wearing the sword on the left. With this conventionality, now seen as meaningless, he contrasts his love for Ruzena, which is beyond all dubious convention. Alienated from the military world, Pasenow becomes increasingly alienated from the civilian world also. He feels himself crushed between the millstones of the civilians, Bertrand and Ruzena, both of whom he finds unreliable, both of whom he considers bad influences. He feels himself losing whatever grip he ever had on the fluid, elusive mass of life. Coming to the conclusion that religion alone can supply the answer, he realizes the gulf that separates him from the freethinker, Bertrand, and the Catholic, Ruzena. Pasenow is being driven into a position of utter solitude. This, indeed, is the central theme of the whole trilogy: "Die Rückverweisung des Menschen auf die Einsamkeit" (22).

Pasenow is relieved when the Sunday service comes round, but the expression on the faces of the soldiers, as they march into the house of God in two parallel columns, is the same expression they wear when exercising or taking riding instruction, without a trace of piety or true feeling. No-one listens to the sermon. Joachim is tempted to call this a circus too. But suddenly a familiar hymn fraught with memories recalls a picture from his youth, a picture of the Holy Family in serene harmony. As a child he had imagined how wonderful it would be to be part of this family. Gradually, however, the picture is transformed, the mother taking on the features of Elisabeth. This Joachim takes to be a sign from God -- he sees the founding of a Christian household with Elisabeth as a kind of earthly counterpart of the Holy Family in the picture, as the answer to his confusion.

After his unfortunate experience with Ruzena, Pasenow feels the gulf between reality and himself widening. He feels himself surrounded by a net of intrigue and iniquity. He imagines Ruzena, the fat gentleman friend, Bertrand to be part of a vast conspiracy of evil. Elisabeth, on the other hand, he comes to see more and more as a symbol of purity in contrast to this web of depravity. He sees it as his responsibility to protect Elisabeth from Bertrand, who, he suspects, is planning to drag her down into the mire. The figure of Helmuth appears to his consciousness, to help him in this task. It seems to him as if Helmuth is taking him by the hand to show him the way back to convention and an ordered existence. Helmuth was, if anything, even more conventional than Joachim, and as the latter retreats more and more into conventional attitudes and separates himself from contemporary reality the figure of Helmuth, who died for a conventional, out-of-date code, naturally springs to mind. Seing Elisabeth, as he does, as a symbol of purity, indeed almost a religious figure (the Romantic gives to the Finite absolute status) Pasenow proposes marriage, in the hope of escaping from the cesspool of iniquity that surrounds him. He tells Bertrand of his proposal, saying how much he fears a rebuff, not for personal reasons but because he sees her acceptance as the only way out of the terrible confusion of the last few months. By her side he believes he can find the way to spiritual freedom and truth. Gradually Elisabeth becomes indistinguishable in his mind from the madonna in his childhood vision.

Shortly before Elisabeth's acceptance death is again near at hand. Joachim, at this moment, understands his father's fear of death and confusedly sees Elisabeth as offering him a means of overcoming death. The passage immediately before this, describing the dissolution of reality into nothingness, is quite remarkable and could be put alongside the most forceful pages of Sartre's "La Nausée" without losing by the comparison:

> die Einsamkeit, die über sie und Joachim verhängt war, war ja hereingebrochen, liess das Gemach trotz seiner traulichen Vornehmheit zu immer grösserer angstvoller Regungslosigkeit erstarren; regungslos sie beide, war es ihnen, als ob um sie der Raum sich weitete und als ob mit den weichenden Wänden die Luft immer dünner und kälter würde, so dünn, dass sie die Stimme kaum mehr trug. Und obwohl alles in Regungslosigkeit erstarrt blieb, schienen die Möbel, schien das Piano, auf dessen schwarzer Lackfläche der Kreis der Gaslichter sich noch spiegelte, nicht mehr an der Stelle zu stehen, wo sie vordem gestanden, sondern weit draussen, und auch die goldenen Drachen und Schmetterlinge auf dem schwarzen chinesischen Paravent in der Ecke waren hinweggehuscht, aufgesaugt gleichsam von den weichenden Wänden, die wie mit schwarzen Tüchern verhängt waren. Die Lichter surrten mit einem kleinen giftigen Pfeifen und neben ihrer winzigen mechanischen Lebendigkeit, die aus unanständig geöffneten schmalen Spalten höhnisch hervorschoss, gab es kein Leben mehr (23).

The first novel of the trilogy ends, as is fitting for a "harmless little story", with a happy ending. Joachim and Elisabeth are married, and we leave them on their wedding night. The marriage, however, is not consummated on this night, Joachim still seeing Elisabeth as a symbol of the Infinite rather than a woman. The description of the painfully inhibited Joachim on his wedding night is one of the funniest parts of the novel. It is a fitting close to the first part of the trilogy, with its relatively light tone and refreshing humour appropriate to the period.

Let us now move on to consider in detail the second novel of the trilogy. "Es wird hierbei vor allem gezeigt", says Broch of the Schlafwandler trilogy,

> dass die Durchsetzung des Lebens mit traumhaften Elementen immer sichtbarer wird, je kraftloser die alten Wert-Traditionen werden. Die "träumerische" Romantik gibt dem Traumhaften weniger Raum als eine Zeit des sachlichen Wertchaos, in der auch das Traumhafte ungebändigt auf sich selbst gestellt ist, selber geradezu sachlich wird (24).

Certainly the difference between "Pasenow" and "Esch oder die Anarchie" is a marked one. The chaos, the anarchy of the epoque, the increasing decline in Western values, is mirrored not only in the chaos of Esch's life but also in the gradual dissolution of the traditional narrative form into a complicated fugue of symbols and associations of images, the invasion of reality by dream-like elements to the point where the boundaries between "reality" and dream are no longer clearly definable. Style and rhythm are intensely animated, almost explosive in their effect, but counterbalanced by reflective passages. When critics speak of expressionism apropos of the "Esch" I feel they are rather wide of the mark. As Broch himself remarks: "die äussere Form naturalistischer Erzählung wird zwar noch beibehalten, aber die innere Bewegtheit spiegelt das Anarchische" (25). I feel that this distinction between form and content is of crucial importance. Broch's purpose in volume two was

> die sozusagen erkenntnistheoretischen Gründe aufzeigen, die, aus dem Boden des Irrationalen (und in zweiter Linie erst Unbewussten) herauswachsend, zu den Ur-Ideen alles Religiösen, der Opferung, der Selbstopferung zur Wiedererlangung des Standes der Unschuld in der Welt führen -- diese religionsphilosophische Grundtendenz, die eigentlich das Philosophische an sich ist, erschien mir in den bisherigen Fassungen zu wenig unterstrichen. Wenn Sie wollen, ist es das Sektierertum mit seinen Verwirrungen, das am Anfang einer jeden Religionsbewegung steht und zu dem (als einem Ausgangspunkt) die Bewegung an ihrem Ende zerfallend zurückkehren muss, m. a. W.: die irrationalen Kräfte, die zur Religionsbildung führen und durch die Kirchlichkeit gebunden werden, werden am Ende der Bewegung wieder frei und entfesselt und nehmen mit gewissen Modifikationen die Formen des Beginns wieder an (26).

August Esch, an accountant, has as his life's motto "business is business". His value-system is that of the book-keeper, the businessman, and he sees the whole world in these terms. He is a "Berufsmensch, aufgefressen von der radikalen Logizität des Wertes, in dessen Fänge er geraten ist", much as Pasenow is. Both Pasenow and Esch see the world in terms of their professional value-system -- for Pasenow the military ethos, for Esch the businessman's ethic. Until Esch's thirtieth year the debits and credits of life seemed to balance, reflecting the orderliness of his books. Then suddenly, on the 2nd March, 1903, he is sacked from his job as accountant. There has been an embezzlement, and Esch is being made the scapegoat, in order to shield someone else. He knows that his books are in perfect order. He is being punished for someone else's mistake. This event shatters Esch's view of the world as a vast account book kept by a divine accountant. Justice has been violated, the world's accounts fraudulently upset. Rather than hand over Nentwig, the guilty man, to the police, Esch blackmails him into giving a model testimonial as the price of his silence. By doing this he incurs a debt of guilt, which must be expiated if the books of life are to be kept straight. If Nentwig is not punished then someone else must suffer. Throughout the novel Esch will try to re-establish the cosmic harmony thus shattered. Everything that happens to Esch is seen by him in the light of the initial imbalance in the books. This is the "irruption from below" in the life of Esch, comparable to the breaking-in of the Irrational in Pasenow's life in the form of the Ruzena experience.

Esch meets by chance Gerneth, the director of a burlesque show, who is advertising the next performance. He obtains free tickets and attends the performance with Balthazar Korn and Erna Korn. What particularly fascinates Esch is an act where a beautiful Hungarian woman, Ilona, is the "target" for her knife-throwing partner. The knife-throwing episode is the first link in a chain of crucifixion symbolism which runs through the work. Broch himself uses the phrase "das gekreuzigte Mädchen" in describing Ilona. Esch feels a kind of ecstasy in imagining himself being "crucified" in Ilona's place (the Freudian death-drive) but a second motif is added: the wish to save Ilona and to sacrifice himself. It is this wish to save another which later plays such an important part, and is the basic religious urge of self-sacrifice. In the depths of the subconscicus Esch feels that sacrifice is necessary to expiate the guilt of the world, to set the cosmic account book straight again for

> ohne Ordnung in den Büchern gab es auch keine Ordnung in der Welt, und so lange keine Ordnung war, würde Ilona weiter den Messern ausgeliefert sein, würde Nentwig sich weiterhin frech und gleissnerisch der Sühne entziehen (27).

Esch and Korn then visit a meeting of the Salvation Army, in the company of the vegetarian and teetotaler Lohberg. Esch has been a victim of solitude since leaving Cologne, realising his solitude and knowing he must die a solitary death. His position is that of Pasenow toward the end of part one, another example of the parallelism of the two parts. "Die Rückverweisung des Menschen auf die Einsamkeit" is indeed the central theme of the trilogy. Feeling as he does, for two pins Esch would have joined the Army in singing the praises of the Lord and the power of divine love, for although Esch is sceptical on the surface, considering the retiring Lohberg to be an idiot and "keuscher Josef", and holds similar views of the Army, nevertheless their message of salvation and of freedom from the fear of death raises echos in the unconscious depths of his being. At this stage, the desire for salvation is not rationally crystallised, but is slumbering in the subconscious, leaving the fear of death still unallayed. Returning to Korn's lodging he enters Erna's room and makes advances to her, only to be rejected. Here again we see the close relatedness of eros and thanatos in the unconscious motivation of Esch. His motives, in entering Erna's room, were in the first place the lustful intentions of the homme moyen sensuel, but behind the erotic drive is the fear of death: lovers hide from each other with their bodies the ghost of death, achieve in the abandonment of self-forgetting a momentary overcoming of death. It is Angst which draws Esch to Erna, a desire for the love which shall stave off death. The real motive behind Esch's action is the desire to overcome thanatos, the crippling loneliness which he had felt since leaving Cologne, the longing of his imprisoned soul for release from solitude.

Broch's account of consciousness is not restricted to the three-dimensionality of the Freudian model (super-ego, ego, id), but includes further dimensions: those dimensions of mind where the fear of death gives rise to the unconscious drive to awakening from the somnambulist state, to salvation and grace. Broch can fairly be said to have advanced beyond Freud, as advances since Freud in the field of "orthodox" psychology (as opposed to behaviorism) have been in this "fourth-dimensional" direction (C.J. Jung). Broch sees not eros but thanatos as the basic human urge. The erotic drive is in fact, in Broch's works, the lowest stage in the overcoming of death, as conditional on the death-drive, and the impression of pessimism left by the "Schlafwandler" is alleviated only later in "Der Versucher" and particularly in his magnum opus, "Der Tod des Vergil", in the vision of Christian agape, which is a true symbol of God's love.

Freud knows only the two basic drives: eros and thanatos. In his strictly scientific attitude Freud does not attempt to go deeper into the question, to find the root of these two drives. After all, his aim was therapeutical, and not philosophical. Broch investigates in his essay on psychoanalysis the common root of these phenomena -- the knowledge of death:

Unter den Erbschaften, die das psychologische Ich in seiner Fühl-Ich-Eigen-
schaft -- fortab soll unter "Ich" stets der gesamte Ich-Komplex einschliess-
lich erkenntnistheoretischen wie psychologischen Denk- und Fühl-Bestandtei-
len verstanden werden -- von seiner rein erkenntnistheoretischen Fassung
übernommen hat, spielt das "Gefühl der Zeitlosigkeit", oder psychologischer
ausgedrückt das "Ewigkeitsgefühl" eine sehr bedeutende Rolle. Im erkenntnistheoretischen Bereich gibt es zwar logische Abfolgen, aber keine Zeit: das
logische Apriori ist mit dem zeitlichen nicht identisch. Mit andern Worten,
der erkenntnistheoretische Ich-Kern, der unverlierbar im Ich sitzt, weiss
nichts von irgendeinem in ihm erfolgenden oder nicht erfolgenden zeitlichen
Ablauf, vielmehr empfindet es sich als eine unveränderliche und unveränder-
bare Einheit, "unsterblich" im wahrsten Wortsinn, und dieses Gefühl zeitloser Unveränderbarkeit ist im psychologischen Ich mit so unverminderter
Stärke erhalten, dass es im Kontakt mit der an und für sich ihm "fremden"
Aussenwelt keinen ihrer Teile so absolut fremd wie eben die Zeit empfindet;
einem Fremdling gleich fühlt sich das Ich in den Zeitstrom hineingehalten,
und von da aus ist es wohl auch zu verstehen, dass das Ich vollkommen un-
fähig ist, sich eine Vorstellung vom eigenen Tod zu machen (28).

For the ego-centre, time belongs to the external world, which is mediated to it
through the empirical layers of the ego, such as the psychological ego and the
physical ego. Although the phenomenon of time is mediated to the ego-centre, it
is close to the ego, for it is closely tied up with the autonomous life of the body-
its pulse-beat, rhythm of breathing, and general organic functions, and the psychological ego, which is affected by this conglommeration of feelings, is aware not
only of the process of these organic functions but also of their termination:

> für das psychologische Ich ist das Zeit-Gefühl, das ihm aus der animalischen
> Sphäre zuflutet, untrennbar mit dem Gefühl des Todes verbunden. Und mit
> dem Tod, den der Mensch von Anbeginn in sich trägt und in sich fühlt, wird
> die Zeit sozusagen zur innersten Aussenwelt (29).

Stripped of the philosophical terminology, this passage is really a modern
reformulation of Platonic or Christian dualism. One might substitute for "Ich-
Kern" "soul" -- that dimension in the structure of consciousness which is beyond
time, but which is conscious of time through the mediation of the animal, organic
functions. Man has, in short, an immortal soul in a mortal body, his body belonging to the external world, his soul a prisoner, a refugee from the Platonic world
or pure forms. Man qua animal being is posessed by a gigantic fear of death, due
to this dualism of consciousness which distinguishes him from the rest of creation.
But precisely from the innermost shrine of the self arises the incohate, as yet
inarticulate striving for release from death and contingency, the irrational, unconscious beginnings of religious feeling. Broch sees our age as an age of transition,
on the threshold of a new feeling toward life, to which the irrational gropings of an
Esch form the overture, much as the irrational, mystical cults of Orphism,
Manichaism, Pythagoreanism formed a prelude to Christianity. Hence Broch
chooses to exemplify these irrational urges in the person of Esch, the simple, ele-
mental average man:

genau so wie die Fischer am See Genezareth keine Intellektuellen waren,
musste ich diesen Menschen wählen ...... weil die religiösen Urtriebe und
Irrationalismen keine Intellektualisierung ihres Werdens und Realisierens
vertragen (30).

Esch attends a union meeting addressed by his friend Martin. Agents provoca-
teurs in the pay of the employers cause the meeting to be broken up and Martin,
who was against the strike, is arrested and later imprisoned. To Esch, this is
further evidence of the evil poisoning the world, further disorder in the cosmic
account book. As everything else, Esch interprets this event in the light of his
initial guilt in not giving Nentwig up to the police. Esch, however, is beginning to
realize that the root cause of the evil in the world is to be sought elsewhere, is
more elusive and remote. He comes to feel that the origin of evil in the world is
something or someone bigger and less accessible than Nentwig. He comes to identify
Bertrand as the source of this evil; the figure of Bertrand gradually replaces that
of Nentwig as arch-villain. Esch's attitude, as that of Pasenow toward Bertrand,
is highly ambivalent. Increasingly, however, he becomes identified with the Anti-
christ in Esch's mind. As the latter walks past the warehouses of the shipping company he sees a vision of Bertrand, more than life-size, a super-murderer, tower-
ing up menacingly, Bertrand the swinish president, who had caused Martin to be
jaoled. And it seems to Esch that he must eliminate this man, not the small fry,
in order to re-establish order in the world. Nentwig is now seen as essentialy
insignificant when Esch meets him at a performance of the ladies' wrestling
matches. He can feel no resentment towards the man who was responsible for his
being fired and considers it useless to hand him over to the police. He is, after
all, only a minor figure compared with Bertrand, who comes more and more to
represent for Esch, if not to embody, the evil in the world.

Esch dreams of a face-to-face encounter with Bertrand, but when the oppor-
tunity presents itself the outcome is not at all what he expected. Bertrand points
out to Esch the futility of killing him or handing him over to the police, in order
to set straight the accounts. He tells him of the impending darkness into which the
world must be plunged before it can become light and pure again, a darkness in
which individuals pursue their solitary destinies like stars in the universe, without
crossing the path of another. In Spite of this meeting with Bertrand, Esch informs
the police of Bertrand's homosexual activities. He is full of satisfaction as he
posts the letter, because the injustice done to Martin has been avenged, the
account set straight.

To atone for his own guilt Esch decides to sacrifice himself. As a first step
he renounces Erna. The fact that he regrets not sleeping with her seems right, and
is in keeping with the idea of sacrifice. Nevertheless, analysing his own feelings,
he sees that by making this small sacrifice he may, in fact, subconsciously be
running away from marriage, and therefore is no better than Nentwig, who also
avoided responsibility. This sacrifice, then, is invalid. Yet sacrifice there must
be if Ilona is not to be exposed to the knives, if Nentwig is not to run around free,
if Martin is not to remain in gaol. Esch searches his mind for a truly significant
outlet for his desire to sacrifice himself. It occurs to him that the others have
given money to the wrestling enterprise. He has no money, but he can offer his
own person, devote his energy and time to the enterprise.

As a first step he will hand in his notice at the shipping firm. He is glad to do this anyhow, since he has no wish to stay with a company responsible for Martin's arrest. Esch goes into partnership with the director Gerneth, who plans to stage ladies' wrestling matches, ostensibly for the prospects of financial gain, but unconsciously to "save" Ilona from her daily "crucifixion" by the knife-thrower. Ilona is to be accommodated in the wrestling circus. The experience of the Salvation Army meeting has taken root in Esch's mind, as also the self-sacrifice of Martin Gehring, who has been imprisoned for political agitation -- a victim of social injustice. "Wer sich opfert ist anständig" he reflects. The concept of self-sacrifice runs through the entire novel. Esch wishes to save Mutter Hentjen -- the human, concrete form, around which his unconscious wishes and phantasies crystallise. Here again, behind self-sacrifice and the impulse to salvation stands thanatos.

This is the insight of the down-at-heels musician Alphonse, who, as a homosexual, as an outsider to the erotic carousel, sees with great objectivity the reality behind the facade of erotic pursuit and love-making. Although Alphonse is but a fat, wretched homosexual, he sees through Esch's failure to fulfill his dreams of salvation, through his self-deception in seeking the Absolute in a human, finite image. This, of course, was Pasenow's error also. He knows that men like Esch are in reality chasing their portion of eternity to protect them from the fear which follows them -- thanatos. They are looking for the Absolute, the Infinite, in earthly form and inevitably find only symbols and substitutes for what they are, in reality, looking for.

Just how accurate an insight into Esch's psyche this is, is shown, in fact, by an examination of Esch's relationship with Mutter Hentjen, which forms the central strand of the second volume, the factual complex, around which a host of unconscious drives and phantasies are crystallised. Esch, who has previously in his batchelor life only pursued fleeting affairs for erotic gratification, sees in Mutter Hentjen, with her fanatical respectability, "etwas Höheres". In contrast to his own confused, tormented mind Mutter Hentjen is a remarkably simple person, knowing quite clearly what is right and wrong, massively confident and sure of her goal in life. It seems to Esch that she is the longed-for harbour in a sea of anarchy and chaos. In fact, however, their relationship is not one of real love and affection, but of erotic attraction. Mutter Hentjen symbolises those unconscious strivings of Esch for self-sacrifice, for something better, for a re-establishing of innocence and justice, crystallised in the dream of "crossing the sea" to America, and starting life anew, as in Esch's attempts to rescue Martin, the political agitator, and re-establish justice.

As throughout the work, the concept of salvation occurs constantly. Esch wishes to save Ilona, Martin, and finally to save Mutter Hentjen from the sordid surroundings in which she works, but also -- and here we see the relevance of the dreams relating to America -- to save her from her past, from the memory of her late husband, from her age-that living portion of death she carries with her:

auch die auszulöschen, deren Mund man sucht, auszulöschen die Zeit, die auch die ihre war, die Zeit, die in den ältlichen Wangen sich niedergelegt hatte, Wunsch, die Frau zu vernichten, die in der Zeit gelebt hatte, zeitlos sie neu erstehen zu lassen, erstarrt und bezwungen in der Vereinigung mit ihm (31)!

Esch's relationship to Mutter Hentjen is of a more stable and mature character than his previous adventures. However, he still remains largely incapable of real communication and enclosed within his ego, his wish to give her a new life in the land beyond the seas being purely egotistical, based on his own fear of death, which he sees held up before him, as in a mirror, in Mutter Hentjen's aged features. In America, thinks Esch, they will be "reborn", the past forgotten. Esch pores over his book on America daily. He is attracted by the fact that the police force in America, according to the book, serves the cause of democratic freedom. It is clear to Esch that in America a flagrant act of injustice, such as Martin's incarceration, would be out of the question. He assiduously learns the English language. It seems, furthermore, to Esch that only in a completely new life, in which the past is totally forgotten, can two people so merge their beings that the past, or for that matter any time, no longer exists for them.

The external reason for the America plans falling through is Gerneth's absconding with the funds. However, there are deeper reasons. America is not a concrete reality for Esch but rather the place beyond the seas where love, innocence and justice exist. The place beyond the seas is not concretely attainable. Esch never really plans to emigrate. It is rather an archetypal symbol of death, as anyone familiar with primitive religion will appreciate. We often refer to death as "the last journey" and, as Freud points out in his "Introductory Lectures on Psycho-analysis" (trans. J. Riviere), dreaming of a journey often conceals the death drive.

The whole relationship of Esch with Mutter Hentjen is based on the plans to emigrate to America, symbolised in the facsimile Statue of Liberty which stands on Mutter Hentjen's shelf-a present from Esch. From the foregoing it will be clear that the torch born by Liberty is one more archetypal symbol of death, and as a motif is taken up at great length in "Der Tod des Vergil". When the America plans fail to materialise the basis of their relationship is withdrawn. This relation-ship was, in any case, based on solitude and creaturely fear, a loneliness which their coming-together could do little to assuage. Each physical act of union leaves them only the more isolated and enclosed in the ego. For this was not the attraction of life for life, but of death for death. It was fear of old age and death which drew Esch to Mutter Hentjen. But Mutter Hentjen is unable to give him what he is looking for; the relationship with her is but an inadequate and finite symbol of that metaphy-sical relation for which Esch, in the depths of consciousness, is striving. At the close of the novel the Salvation Army again appears on the scene as a memento mori, admonishing Esch to save his soul in receiving the doctrine of redemption, structurally showing how far Esch has progressed spiritually since his first encounter with the Army, and yet how far he still is from a true understanding of self and of his metaphysical fear. They are "idiots" for him, and yet, in his divided mind, he concedes that they are possibly right in singing of the imprisoned soul which is freed by the power of redeeming love. He admits that they might be right in thinking that the highest goal in life consists in finding the way to true, complete love or agape.

If Esch rejects the spiritual message of salvation from death, from sin and evil -- for in Broch's words "Der Tod ist der absolute Unwert" -- with his mind, on a purely conscious plane, his experiences in the course of the second part of the trilogy have brought him to a spiritual point where he is, in the depths of his consciousness, more in agreement with this doctrine than he would consciously admit. It is logically necessary, or rather necessary within the peculiar logic of the work of art, that he should, in the third novel of the trilogy, become a sectarian lay-preacher in his activities as newspaper editor and leader, with Pasenow, of a death-centered religious sect.

Apart from the basic "sleepwalker" imagery, there are a number of symbols of modern man's spiritual predicament to be found in part two of the trilogy. At one point Broch compares the characters to puppets manipulated by an unseen, remote puppet-master. Man is also seen as a prisoner, the symbols of imprisonment running through the three parts of the trilogy, and a cripple, Martin Gehring and Lieutenant Jaretzki being representatives of the human condition. And finally the symbol of the orphan: Esch is an orphan. He seeks consolation and fulfilment with "Mutter" Hentjen. To him, the orphan, the finding of the mother-figure means security at last. In a wider sense, Esch and twentieth-century people generally are spiritual orphans, without a spiritual heritage, without the security of fixed, settled values, caught between yesterday and tomorrow. Broch finds yet another expression of the twentieth century predicament in the symbol of travelling:

> Die Reisenden hingegen und die Waisenkinder, sie alle, die die Brücken hinter sich verbrennen, wissen nicht mehr, wie es um sie steht. In die Freiheit geworfen, müssen sie Ordnung und Gerechtigkeit neu errichten; .... (32)

Although they reject the reality of the world around them, like Esch the sleepwalkers are incapable of summoning the awful revolution of knowledge in which two and two no longer make four. This last phrase is a clear reference to Esch's bookkeeping concepts. Esch, like Pasenow, hides in a conventional value-system which protects him from life. The only hope for man, however, is to leave behind conventional ways of life and thought and try to attain a new vision of life. Until then, modern man will be isolated, alone in an alien world with no recognisable landmarks to orientate himself, like an orphan. In the dream section, where Esch has a vision of the "promised land", yet another image is used to describe the spiritual position of modern man-that of the colonist. The colonists, in Esch's dream, have left behind the old world (of traditional European values) and settled in a virgin land. But they do not feel at home; they restlessly travel the steppes in their cars, driven on by an insatiable longing. Even when they "settle down" in the sense of building a home, they feel themselves to be aliens in an alien world. Their yearning is directed toward the future, but a future which will for ever remain future, ever unattainable. Esch is very much in this position. He realizes that the solution he has found in the relationship with Mutter Hentjen is not a final one, "Ziel, das er Liebe nennt und das wie ein letzterreichbarer fester Punkt der Küste vor dem Unerreichbaren steht" (33). It is far removed from that final goal where symbol and original image are resolved to unity (34). At the very end of the second part Esch has a glimpse of the future way to that goal and realizes the futility of his previous attempts to seek salvation from death, fulfilment and freedom in the real world.

Esch comes to realize that his dream of going across the sea to America, even if it had materialized, would not have brought him satisfaction. He realizes that this way is only the symbol of a higher way which one must go, just the earthly image of that higher way which we see as through a glass darkly. If such words had featured in his vocabulary Esch would have spoken of the spiritual sphere in which alone fulfilment, the Absolute is to be sought. Such ideas are beyond him, but he recognises that his old book-keeping concept of life was a fraud. He now sees earthly things from a higher standpoint, as if he were looking down on the plain of life from a tall castle. The events of part two are now seen as very much part of the past which Esch determinedly puts behind him, as he resolutely looks toward the future; they seem as unreal as a scene on a dimly-lit stage, a play which is forgotten and never really there. Esch realises the futility of seeking fulfilment in the here-and-now:

> der Weg der Sehnsucht und der Freiheit ist unendlich und niemals ausschreit-bar, ist schmal und abseitig wie der des Schlafwandlers, wenn es auch der Weg ist, der in die geöffneten Arme der Heimat führt und an ihre atmende Brust (35).

Esch and Mutter Hentjen marry and sell the public house, actions which are "Stationen auf dem Wege der Annäherung an das Höhere und Ewige" (36).

The chapters centering around Huguenau form the central narrative strand of the third volume of the trilogy. The two main characters of the previous volumes, Pasenow and Esch, are also co-protagonists in the Huguenau chapters.

The external action is straightforward enough. Huguenau, stationed at the front, one day becomes aware of the absurdity of war, and of his role in the war, and deserts. By so doing he cuts himself off from the conventional social framework, inside which desertion is a punishable crime, and asserts his freedom. Herein lies the importance of Huguenau within the framework of the novel: he represents freedom from the old, decaying values which Pasenow and Esch still cling to. He is the one character who looks to the future. Pasenow and Esch are both subject to moral dogmas which are in decline and therefore become the material for romanticism. Bertrand tries to escape from the harsh realities of life into a world of aesthetic delights beyond Good and Evil:

> Bloss Huguenau ist der wahrhaft "wertfreie" Mensch und damit das adäquate Kind seiner Zeit. Er allein kann daher fortbestehen, er allein ist in der "Autonomie dieser Zeit", in der sich ein revolutionäres Ringen nach Freiheit ausdrückt. Er ist der passive Revolutionär, wie eben die Masse der Revolutionäre jede Revolution passiv mitmacht und doch macht. Sicherlich hat er -- bloss der Form des Autonomen nach ethisch, sonst aber völlig amoralisch -- noch keineswegs die Freiheit der neuen Göttlichkeit, des neuen Glaubens errungen; er erstrebt dies auch gar nicht, ersehnt es auch nicht, obwohl hie und da ein Lichtblick kommender Möglichkeiten in ihm aufzuckt: genau so wie diese Zeit noch nicht ihre Gläubigkeit gefunden hat, noch lange nicht finden wird, sondern nur hie und da ahnt (37).

And so, as Huguenau finds himself in a mediaeval German town for the first time he takes time off to appreciate its aesthetic charm. He had, in the course of his business travels, visited many such a town before but had previously been blind to such things. Huguenau is seized by a strange feeling. If anyone had told him

that this was a feeling for beauty or a feeling originating from freedom, he would
have ridiculed the idea. But he would be wrong

> da auch für ihn ein tieferes menschliches Wissen, ein menschliches Sehnen
> nach einer Freiheit vorhanden sein muss, in der alles Licht der Welt an-
> hebt und aus der die Heiligung des Lebendigen sonntäglich aufspriesst, --
> und weil dies so ist und weil dies nicht anders sein kann, so mag es wohl
> auch in jenem Augenblick geschehen sein, in dem Huguenau aus dem Graben
> kroch und sich erstmalig der menschlichen Verbundenheit entlöste, dass
> ein Schimmer des höheren Glanzes, der die Freiheit ist, auf ihn fiel, auch
> ihm zuteil wurde, und er in diesem Augenblick zum ersten Male dem Sonntag
> geschenkt war (38).

Despite his newly won freedom, once he settles in the town Huguenau's commercial instincts reassert themselves. He decides to buy up Esch's newspaper
by fraudulent methods, and to cover this fraud he approaches Pasenow and informs
him that certain influential and patriotic industrialists have entrusted him with the
task of taking over certain newspapers which disseminate corrupt ideas among the
people. He refuses to mention their names, thereby cleverly hinting that men of
considerable stature are involved. The "Kurtriersche Bote", he tells Pasenow,
is one such newspaper, and should be bought as soon as possible, to prevent the
people being corrupted by its ideas. As it happens, the circumstances favour
Huguenau, for Esch is finding the position of editor incompatible with his personality
and his accountant's neat and tidy view of how the world should be. The gulf between
Esch's vision of reality and actual reality, which we observed in volume two, has
now become sharply focussed, as Esch struggles with the task of keeping the
world's books in order in a time of war when unpredictability, disorder and chaos
are the order of the day. He has trouble with the censors. More and more, as an
editor, he becomes "ein hagerer Ritter, der mit seiner eingelegten Lanze Angriff
um Angriff reiten muss zu Ehren der Rechnung, die in der Welt glatt aufgehen
soll" (39). So, when Huguenau casually mentions the possibility of selling the
paper, Esch is interested from the start. Huguenau, of course, being the complete
businessman, conceals his interest, and starts by pointing out the drawbacks.
Although he has never seen a printing machine before he criticises the machine for
its antiquated design.

Faced with the problem of raising capital, Huguenau turns to local business
interests. Here again he shows his commercial astuteness: he resists the temptation
to ask them for the full amount. If he did so, someone might ask him for proof of
his good faith. However, he reasons, if he refuses too high a share and insists on
keeping the majority share for his own fictitious group then nobody will doubt that
he is, in fact, the representative of the biggest and richest industrial group in
Germany. And in fact they do believe him. Having told the group that the price is
20'000, Huguenau will now try to knock Esch down to 14'000, leaving himself a
clear profit of 6'000. With this scheme in mind Huguenau visits Esch in his office.
He tells Esch how shocked he has been by the negative criticisms he has heard of
the newspaper. Even though he is, he claims, a disinterested outsider it breaks
his heart to see a good newspaper ruined. A newspaper depends on its reputation,
and when that is tarnished the paper is as good as ruined. Thanks to Esch the news-

paper is virtually unsellable, in fact Esch should pay someone to take it off his hands rather than have the effrontery to ask money for it. Fortunately, Huguenau continues, a group of self-sacrificing men have offered, thanks to his disinterested mediation, to take over the paper at the price of 10'000. Suavely Huguenau talks Esch into signing a contract, according to which he, Esch, remains in posession of 10 % and 30 % goes to the group of local interests and 60 % to the group of industrialists represented by Huguenau. Huguenau will bring to the enterprise a capital sum of DM 20'000, of which a third will be paid initially. The other two-thirds are to be paid in six months or a year. In point of fact, of course, Huguenau himself is paying nothing. The third share is paid by the group of local interests. The rest need not be paid for another year, and in times of war who knows what can happen in a year? The DM 6'600 is duly paid by the group of local interests. DM 4'000 Huguenau gives to Esch; DM 1'600 is kept for expenses, and the remaining DM 100 Huguenau keeps for himself.

The relationship between Esch and Huguenau gradually deteriorates. Huguenau partly sees Esch, no doubt, as a commercial rival, and therefore someone to be destroyed. But also, thematically, it is necessary that Huguenau, the "wertfreier Mensch", the forerunner of the New Man if not the New Man himself, should attempt to destroy Esch, who clings to the old values. He writes a letter to Major Pasenow, accusing Esch of associating with subversive elements in the town and of entertaining revolutionary views himself.

For various reasons, however, Esch and Pasenow, the representatives of the old order, have grown closer to each other. V. Pasenow has become disillusioned by the war. This war is no longer a matter of colourful, romantic uniforms, of gentleman soldiers who fought according to the rules of chivalry. The war had not proved to be the hoped-for crowning glory of his military career and past life, but had, on the contrary, undermined the very foundations of this life. It had revealed the presence of evil in the world -- a quantity which the intellectual resources learned in the cadet school could not cope with. From the ensuing struggle in Pasenow's soul arises the concept, or rather the dream of a civitas dei as a solution. "Und so zog sich eine zwar verschwommene und manchmal verzerrte, aber immerhin verfolgbare Linie von Zeno und Seneca, vielleicht sogar schon von den Pythagoräern bis zu den Gedankengängen des Majors v. Pasenow", comments Broch drily (40). This is, of course, a further example of v. Pasenow's romanticism, as is his embracing of Lutheranism, in other words a dead system of dogmas belonging to the past. Like every other Romantic, v. Pasenow cannot accept the present. Esch, on the other hand, has his own mystical interpretation of religion. The following passage from the epilogue to "Die Schlafwandler" is of great interest as helping to elucidate Esch's condition and also as the germ of Broch's ideas on mass-psychology, which were later to find definitive form in the "Bergroman" and the "Massenpsychologie":

> Gross ist die Angst des Menschen, der sich seiner Einsamkeit bewusst wird und aus seinem eigenen Gedächtnis flüchtet; ein Bezwungener und Ausgestossener ist er, zurückgeworfen in tiefste kreatürliche Angst, in die Angst dessen, der Gewalt erleidet und Gewalt tut, und zurückgeworfen in eine übermächtige Einsamkeit, kann seine Flucht und seine Verzweiflung und seine Dumpfheit so gross werden, dass er daran denken muss, sich ein Leid anzu-

tun, dem steinernen Gesetz des Geschehens zu entrinnen. Und in der Furcht vor der Stimme des Gerichtes, die aus dem Dunkel hervorzubrechen droht, erwacht in ihm mit doppelter Stärke die Sehnsucht nach dem Führer, der leicht und milde bei der Hand ihn nimmt, ordnend und den Weg weisend, der Führer, der keinem mehr nachfolgt und der vorangeht auf der unbeschrittenen Bahn des geschlossenen Ringes, aufzusteigen zu immer höheren Ebenen, aufzusteigen zu immer hellerer Annäherung, er, der das Haus neu erbauen wird, damit aus Totem wieder das Lebendige werde, er selber auferstanden aus der Masse der Toten, der Heilsbringer, der in seinem eigenen Tun das unbegreifbare Geschehen dieser Zeit sinnvoll machen wird, auf dass die Zeit neu gezählt werde (41).

The difference between Esch's mystical religiosity and Pasenow's acceptance of conventional Protestantism is brought out in the dramatic scene between Esch, Frau Esch, v. Pasenow and Huguenau. Stylistically the form of this scene helps, together with a host of other instances, to break up the traditional novel form. In Broch's introductory comment, however, we also realize that the dramatic form represents yet another variation on the sleepwalker symbol: we all play roles on the stage which we call the world.

The first signs of social unrest manifest themselves -- the social counterpart to the chaos of the war outside. As Esch and Pasenow are passing the town jaol, they hear a strange buzzing sound. Suddenly the town commandant's car arrives. The buzzing becomes louder and they recognise the word "hunger" repeated over and over again in a rhythmic chant. This revolt of the prisoners is put down but, soon after, this revolutionary mood finds echos in the world outside the prison gates. A march on the prison is organized. Huguenau is sympathetic to their revolutionary mood and goes with them. In fact he feels like a general in charge of an army. The mob break down the prison gates, Huguenau executing the first blow, symbolising his opposition to the old order and underlining his position in the book. The mob throng into the courtyard, only to find it deserted. The prison staff have gone into hiding. Huguenau sees this little revolution as a triumph over Pasenow and Esch, and so it is, insofar as the latter represent the old order. The mob then get out of hand and violence breaks out. Buildings are set on fire and a warder is brutally beaten. Huguenau's contribution to the violence is to rape Frau Esch. "In gewissem Sinn ist Huguenau damit auch der eigentliche Gegenspieler Mutter Hentjens geworden", writes Broch in a letter to the Rhein-Verlag," -- daher auch, von aller psychologischer Motivation abgesehen, die Notwendigkeit seiner Kopulierung mit ihr --, Mutter Hentjens, die ihrerseits von allem Anbeginn "wertfrei" und autonom ist" (42). With deft, economical brush-strokes Broch conjures up a scene of violence of almost hallucinatory power, by concentrating on significant detail in the general chaos and violence and thereby better suggesting this chaos and horror than by dwelling at length on the whole scene:

Aus einer Seitengasse schwankte ihm ein Mann entgegen, der ein Fahrrad führte: mit der Linken hielt er die Lenkstange umkrampft, die Rechte hing, wie gebrochen, schlotternd herab; Huguenau sah mit Grausen in ein zerschlagenes, zerschmettertes Gesicht, aus dem noch ein Auge blicklos ins Leere starrte (43).

As a final touch to this fresco of violence, Huguenau murders Esch. Broch describes Huguenau as "einen fast verbrecherischen Typus, der seinen Kindheitstraum in der Wirklichkeit einfach naiv zu Ende lebt" (44). On the psychological level Huguenau lives out his Oedipus complex, kills the father-figure Esch and sleeps with "mother" Esch. On a deeper level the murder of Esch by Huguenau symbolises the process of revolution in the context of the decline of western values:

> immer ist es so, dass der Mensch des kleineren Wertverbandes den Menschen des sich auflösenden grösseren Verbandes vernichtet, immer übernimmt er, der Unglücklichste, die Rolle des Henkers im Prozess des Wertzerfalls, und an dem Tage, an dem die Fanfaren des Gerichtes ertönen, dann ist es der wertfreie Mensch, der zum Henker einer Welt wird, die sich selbst gerichtet hat (45).

The major having been injured in this orgy of violence, Huguenau offers to transport him by ambulance to Cologne. The doctors, short-staffed and harrassed, have no option but to agree. With a red cross on his sleeve and on the ambulance he is sure of a safe passage with no questions asked. Huguenau delivers the major to the hospital in Cologne, sees that he is taken care of, and then secures from the hospital authorities a military travel pass to Colmar, his home. There remained only one thing to do before leaving: the next morning Huguenau withdrew the remaining capital belonging to the newspaper from the bank, and then left. As a ruthless businessman, however, he is not content with this, and writes to Frau Esch, suggesting selling back to her the share in the newspaper which was never his in the first place. The fraud is successful. "Das war eine erpresserische und hässliche Handlung", comments the author, "aber sie wurde von Huguenau nicht als solche empfunden; sie verstiess weder gegen seine Privattheologie noch gegen die des kommerziellen Wertsystems" (46).

What exactly does Huguenau stand for? Broch gives us several indications in the epilogue. With the break-up of the European value-system, both the rational elements in life and the irrational elements are unleashed and run riot. The all-embracing religious system places everything in the world in a rational perspective; when this system begins to disintegrate the irrational elements, in particular, are no longer harnessed and creatively chanelled by an all-enveloping system. The last unit in this decline of values is the human individual. The less the individual participates in a comprehensive value-system and the more he is left to his own empirical autonomy, the smaller and more limited becomes his "private theology", and the less capable the latter of incorporating any values outside its own narrow sphere. Modern man, cast out of the community of a central value-system, metaphysically homeless, because this community has dissolved into a conglommeration of individuals, is without values, without style and irrationally motivated:

> Huguenau, ein wertfreier Mensch, gehörte allerdings auch dem kommerziellen System an; er war ein Mann, der in Branchekreisen einen guten Ruf genoss, er war ein gewissenhafter und umsichtiger Kaufmann und er hatte seiner kaufmännischen Pflicht stets voll und ganz, ja, mit aller Radikalität Folge geleistet. Dass er Esch umgebracht hatte, fiel zwar nicht in den kaufmännischen Pflichtenkreis, widersprach aber nicht dessen Usancen. Es war

eine Art Ferialhandlung gewesen, getätigt zu einer Zeit, in welcher auch
das kaufmännische Wertsystem aufgehoben und bloss das individuelle übrig-
gebliebten war (47).

Huguenau had committed a murder; afterwards he forgot about it entirely. On the
other hand, he remembered every single commercial success of his career. His
value-system is the commercial value-system and only those actions which fit into
the scheme of this value-system are considered worthy of note. As it happens,
Huguenau remains a businessman, within the commercial value-system. However,
he might just as easily have become an equally successful revolutionary in different
circumstances. For actually there is no such thing as a "revolutionary". And
certainly the proletarian, the instrument of the revolution, is not a revolutionary
in this sense. The proletarian revolution is just a part of the larger social and
cultural process of valuative disintegration. The proletarian is the exponent of the
modern european spirit, the spirit of positivism and dissolution of values which is
spreading across the whole of the West. Broch does not see the revolutionary movement in Marxist terms, but rather as a confirmation of his theories on the decline
of the West.

Even Huguenau becomes, in later years, infected by the valuative vacuum of
the times. Even his partial system (the commercial) no longer exercises its power.
He feels deeply isolated and yet he has a glimmering of the future community which
must, in time, supercede our epoque of despair and alienation. The dim knowledge
of this future community alienates him from his surroundings, although in his
general behaviour and way of life he is in no way different from his fellows and
seems to be the epitome of the solid merchant type. The world of men and human
preoccupations becomes increasingly remote as he strives for the goal of truth,
ultimate reality. It is in this striving for truth that Huguenau's drive to freedom,
with its dire consequences in his life hitherto, is justified. The freedom of the
self is, after all, a reflection of the Platonic freedom of God. Although he knows
the goal is unattainable he will strive for it,

> den Weg zu durchschreiten, der wie eine Kreisbahn zu immer höheren
> Ebenen ansteigt und auf dem das Gewesene und Versinkende als höheres
> Ziel wieder aufersteht, um mit jedem Schritte zurückzusinken in die ferne-
> ren Nebel: unendliche Bahn des geschlossenen Ringes und der Vollendung,
> luzide Realität, in der die Dinge zerfallen und auseinanderrücken bis zu den
> Polen und bis an die Grenzen der Welt, wo alles Getrennte wieder eins wird,
> wo die Entfernung wieder aufgehoben ist und das Irrationale seine sichtbare
> Gestalt annimmt, wo Furcht nicht mehr zu Sehnsucht, Sehnsucht nicht mehr
> zu Furcht wird, wo die Freiheit des Ichs wieder in die platonische Freiheit
> Gottes mündet, unendliche Bahn des geschlossenen Ringes und der Vollendung,
> für den nur beschreitbar, der sein Wesen erfüllt hat, -- unerreichbar für
> jeden (48).

In our times of cultural decline and revolution this goal is unattainable. Even
if Huguenau had settled for the revolutionary value-system, instead of the commercial, the way of fulfilment would have been closed to him. For although Huguenau
has forgotten the murder of Esch, the exploitation of Frau Esch and countless other
evil deeds, these deeds remain despicable. In fact what Huguenau stands for --

a value-system which does not transcend the individual and his irrational drives -- is the absolute zero-point, the final product of the decline of values. It seems to be almost a law in the process of cultural decline that this zero-point of the disintegration of values must come before mankind glimpses the rising star of freedom and new values. Corrupt and unscrupulous though he is, Huguenau's actions throughout the novel may all be explained by the drive to freedom. We have already mentioned that Huguenau stands for freedom, albeit on a small scale. Even if he only attains the freedom of the murderer, by killing Esch, of the deserter, by leaving the front line, it is nevertheless freedom of a kind. And thus he represents an extremely important idea and herolds the future. In the idea of freedom lies the justification and hope of a renewal of humanity and values. Although freedom is a platonic idea, an unattainable Absolute, mankind has the duty of for ever renewing its attempts to reach it. This ever-renewed attempt Broch calls the "Revolution der Erkenntnis", a revolution which must be undertaken if the decadence of the old value-system is to be followed by the birth of a new system.

The minor plots are all variations on the same theme: the decline of values and the consequent alienation of modern man. The Maurer Goedicke chapters show an extreme, physical case of alienation. The Jaretzki chapters show Broch in a satirical vein, revealing the absurdity of war with a macabre humour and bitter pointedness reminiscent of Karl Kraus. Jaretzki himself has been shocked to the depths of his being by having to kill his fellow man. He does not know what he has been fighting for. He is for ever telling the doctors and the sister that the war will never end, and for him it will not, for the war is but the most dramatic expression of the anarchy and metaphysical homelessness of our times. "So richtig nach Hause kommt keiner mehr" (49). Maybe he will actually return home in the literal sense, but his faith in the moral order has been irrecoverably lost. He is, as Ziolkowski points out, a personification of the spiritual imbalance of the age: "an architect by profession (that is, a symbol of proportion), who has lost an arm and must now get used to an artificial limb" (50).

The Hannah Wendling chapters trace her growing loneliness. The ostensible cause of this loneliness is her separation from her husband, who is at the Eastern Front, but the real cause lies much deeper. Her alienation is a product of the decline of values. Hannah Wendling is described as leading a life devoid of substance. In fact her relationship to what one calls "life" was very tenuous. She shuns the company of her fellow human beings. Her alienation goes so far that when she awoke in the night she could hardly believe that it was her child sleeping in the next room. Her alienation assumes extreme proportions, going so far as to include her own physical existence: when she plays the piano it seems to her that someone else's hands are playing. She begins to forget her husband's name. Her spiritual alienation stands in contrapuntal relationship to the physical alienation of Maurer Goedicke.

The Heilsarmeemädchen chapters are a further variation on the same theme. For Broch the Salvation Army is a sign of religious decadence. The actions of the Salvation Army girl are seen as heroic but totally meaningless. She and the chapters centered upon her are a further elaboration of the main theme of loneliness. The narrator, Bertrand Müller, Dr. Phil., sees through the facade of hymn singing of Marie and Nuchem to the existential void behind. In these chapters

we are introduced to yet another symbol of modern man's predicament in the figure
of Ahasver, the wandering Jew:

> im Todesraume schwebe ich,
> schreiend und ewig, Ahasver!
> Im schlaflosen blutgelben Höllenlicht,
> verdorrt meine Hände, verdorrt mein Gesicht,
> zum Schreien geboren, ich, Ahasver!
> Verjagt aus dem Ursprung, in Klüfte gejagt,
> im Wissen erhoben, im Zweifel zernagt,
> Steine aussäend, vom Staube genährt,
> ans Wissen geschmiedet, im Sehnen verzehrt,
> von Stimmen gesegnet, von der Stimme verflucht,
> gesegneter Sämann der verbotenen Frucht (51).

The chapters forming the "Zerfall der Werte" provide both a commentary on
the various episodes of the trilogy and a philosophico-sociological basis for the
entire trilogy, explaining the predicament of the characters and their motivation
in a way which transcends the psychological novel. As printed in the Schlafwandler
they form part of the intricate counterpoint of the trilogy, of the "musical" structure which characterises Broch as an artist. Placed together, they form a valuable
philosophical contribution to the understanding of the modern era and modern man's
relationship to knowledge and truth.

Modern man lives in a perpetual twilight zone, a state of somnambulism, of
unreality, in which the only reality is his gigantic death-wish, the emptiness and
meaninglessness of life. Broch brilliantly analyses in the "Zerfall der Werte" the
process of decline from the monotheistic cosmogony of the Middle Ages to the
chaos of values which have become autonomous, each claiming absoluteness. Broch
sees the Renaissance as the starting point of the five-hundred year long dissolution
of values, a time in which the Christian value-system was sundered into the rival
forces of Catholicism and Protestantism, in which the mediaeval organon was
dissolved.

For Broch the form of logic remains the same at all times. Only the contents
of thought change, the potentially infinite processes of thought being only limited
by the concept of plausibility, which varies between different cultures and stages
of culture. Within the cosmological scheme of mediaeval culture all questions, all
chains of reasoning terminate in the idea of God. Now, with the dissolution of this
culture, cosmogony no longer rests on God and his divinity but on the infinite per-
petuation of questioning. Man's logical activity is limited by no point of plausibility,
but he is thrown into the Infinite, an infinity of uncertainty and doubt, the infinite
of vacuity.

Whereas mediaeval culture posessed a central value-concept under which all
other values were subsumed-the Christian belief in God -, a world-order which was
the image of eternal and infinite harmony, man himself in all his activities belonging to this harmonious whole, every schere of activity, every department of life
given meaning and direction by reference to a central value determining cultural
unity, each reality, however mundane, symbolic of a higher reality, a finitely
infinite chain of symbols terminating in God, the noumenal ground of Being, of

whose divine reality all symbols are but the finite reflections, the Platonic mind before its incorporation in the world of spatio-temporality, now the ground has been shifted from the finite infinity of a God still anthropomorphically conceived to truly abstract infinity. The mediaeval world-view was grounded in Being, not Becoming, in multidimensionality, whereas the modern world is given up to the three-dimensional world of Becoming, of the certainty of death.

Whereas the mediaeval artist knew only service of the faith, placing his skill and technique at the disposal of that faith and the mediaeval merchant and soldier acted in the service of the only absolute value-faith-, in the Faustian age each separate sphere of value has acquired the status of absolute validity and is no longer subordinated to a central value at the apex of a valuative hierarchy reflecting divine order. Each sphere of activity pursues its own logic, its own ethos, without reference to the moral norms and limitations imposed by the central value. The same applies to the intellectual as to the businessman, artist, scholar, soldier.

The very existence of the modern intellectual is a symptom of the decline of the Platonic world-concept. Within the totality of a purely spiritual world-order, as represented by Platonic-Christian culture, there is no place for the modern intellectual. The proof of God's existence presumes the doubt of God's existence and is an individual attempt to come to terms with the divine system as such. The existence of the modern intellectual with his tragic isolation is a sign of religious-cultural disintegration. For religion means precisely re-ligio, a binding-together, a harbouring, an encompassing. Cast out from this harbouredness, from this "Geborgenheit", modern man is thrown upon himself, thrown into the void of infinite questionings, certain only of his ultimate mortality. For everything that bears the name "religious" is a coming-to-terms with death.

Religion transforms the world into a spiritual cosmogony, subordinates it under the Platonic logos; taking upon itself the task of liberating the world from the stranglehold of chance and contingency, it aims to be a release from the constraint of the empirical, release from the most terrible constraint to which the human soul is subjected: mortality. The religious state is the state of freedom from constraint, of Grace. With the break-up of such a Platonic world-view the intellectual in his tragic isolation becomes the bearer of the Platonic Idea, of reason and of freedom. And yet the intellectual cannot avoid sharing to some extent the sceptical, positivistic spirit of the age, a spirit which dismisses all deductive and speculative philosophy, in fact all philosophy in so far as its concern is metaphysical or ethical, as mere aesthetic play or "mysticism", in an age which is, in short, truly unphilosophical.

This positivistic spirit restricts itself to the language of things, rather than the language of God. Individual disciplines are born to study individual fields of study, a system of parallel and separate fields of value exist as regards knowledge itself, a development which runs parallel to our earlier consideration of the changed status of the artist, merchant, soldier. There exist the value-systems of the scientist, historian, scholar which run parallel and have become absolute, only relate to themselves and within the sphere of reference of the profession or field of knowledge in question and do not relate to any value transcending that sphere of reference. We have a chaos of parallel and contending values not unified by any cultural centre, which cannot hide the void engulfing modern man.

Parallel to this chaos of secular value-systems is the appearance in modern times of a host of religious sects -- a further sign of cultural decline. Protestantism adopts an attitude of toleration toward extra-religious fields of value, and not of incorporation. Religion no longer attempts to infuse these extra-religious fields with religious and Platonic content. This is one more example of the decomposition of the central Catholic value-system. Just as we have the attitude of business is business, l'art pour l'art, war is war, so we now have what Broch calls, "Religion an sich" a purely individual and immediate, an existential apprehension of God based on pure intuition, unsupported by any cosmogony, any comprehensive attempt to meaningfully penetrate life in all its aspects with a Platonic vision of order. Thus the "immediacy" of the Protestant experience of God is parallel to the immediacy of the empirical/scientific approach to reality, both unmediated by any comprehensive philosophy or scheme of values, both dealing directly with the "facts" of immediate experience. Hence Broch sees the unity of the Renaissance and the Reformation -- one of the strongest points in his argument. Behind the ascetic severity of Protestantism stands the fear and trembling of modern man exposed to the cold winds of the Absolute, infinitely removed from God in the infinitude of his experience, undertaking in the dark night of the soul the mystical flight of the alone to the alone, no longer carried and harboured by a unified world-order, accomplishing individually that overcoming of death which is the basic drive, making the leap of faith across the abyss, re-establishing his freedom. Modern man is faced with an empty heaven, a silent God. He is infinitely removed from God, Kafka's K. in his attempts to reach communication with the castle, crippled by insecurity and fear of the abstract cruelty of the Absolute.

The anthropomorphic God of the finitely infinite Trinity has become the God whose name is no longer to be pronounced and of whom no images can be made, remote in the neutral infinity of the Absolute, a remote God whose messages no longer reach man, who dwells unreachable in the Castle of the Grail. Such is the Götterferne of our age. Yet it is of no avail to bury one's head in the sand, to seek refuge in a romantically idealised mediaevalism -- that is Pasenow's error. The cultural unity of the Middle Ages is lost beyond recall. One must have the courage to be, one must face the icy blast of the Absolute, the ever-threatening void, face reality and fulfill man's duty of seeking truth, Erkenntnis, thereby showing the truth of the saying that God created man in his own image. But this involves standing naked before life and death. Pasenow's uniform shuts him off from the exposedness of life, just as his flight into traditional religion provides an escape from the twentieth-century predicament, and is ultimately lacking in honesty.

In "Huguenau" the chaos of society, the complete disintegration of the old order, is reflected in the shattering of the traditional novel form. We have, it is true, a central narrative but the traditional laws of causation and psychological motivation are not to be found. And the various chapters of the Huguenau narrative are split up and contrapuntally juxtaposed with other sub-narratives to form a dense fugal texture. All these narratives are variations on the main theme. Narrative prose suddenly gives way to philosophical essay; lyric poetry is succeeded by aphorisms and suddenly the whole thing is dissolved into dramatic form. If nothing else, then Broch certainly demonstrated in the "Schlafwandler" an astonishing literary virtuosity in his mastery of these various literary forms. Broch was, in fact, aiming at a revolutionary novel form, in the belief that new knowledge can only be gained through new form.

The fact that the role of the modern novel consists in gaining new knowledge is a result of the present situation in the sciences and philosophy, according to Broch. With increasing specialisation science and philosophy are no longer capable of embracing the whole of life and the whole of knowledge. This task is now for the novel to fulfill. The novel must now represent the totality of life. To do this the novel requires a multi-dimensional form transcending the old naturalistic technique. Man must be portrayed in the totality of his experience, from the physical and emotional levels to the moral and metaphysical. This was Broch's objective in writing "Die Schlafwandler". He sees the novel as a first attempt to achieve the "epistemological novel", which he sees as the goal of his art.

The novel has taken over the task of dealing with those areas of philosophy which fulfill metaphysical needs but are rejected by "philosophers" at the present as "unscientific" and not belonging to philosophy. The polyhistoric novel is the ideal vehicle for fulfilling this role. The main problem in this novel form, however, has been the artistic assimilation of the philosophical and poetic elements. The choice of philosophers, intellectuals or scientists as protagonists or the use of learned dialogue to transmit the philosophical content is extremely artificial and destroys poetic unity. According to Broch Gide, Musil, Thomas Mann and Aldous Huxley are all guilty of this artificiality and superficiality, this failure to find a suitable new form:

> Bei den meisten dieser Autoren steht die Wissenschaft, steht die Bildung wie ein kristallener Block neben ihrem eigentlichen Geschäft, und sie brechen einmal dieses Stückchen, ein andermal jenes Stückchen davon ab, um ihre Erzählung damit aufzuputzen (52).

In his own work Broch claims to have found a quite different solution:

> Nun meine Methode: so gerne ich sie mit Joyce vergliche, weiss ich meine Grenzen. Aber ich weiss auch, dass der "Zerfall" (den man freilich nicht alleine nehmen darf, vielmehr bildet er mit der Gesamtmethode des Huguenau ein Ganzes) einen wesentlichen und originalen Schritt zum polyhistorischen Roman darstellt. Ueber die Schichtenkonstruktion habe ich der gnädigen Frau schon geschrieben. Und nun wäre nur noch dazu zu sagen, dass das Wissenschaftliche eben nicht als Gesprächsfüllsel verwendet wird, sondern als oberste rationale Schicht mitschwimmt und mitschwingt. Es ist also ganz ausgeschlossen, den "Zerfall" anders einzugliedern, als es geschehen ist. Ganz abgesehen davon, dass er in fortlaufender Kontrapunktik zu der "Heilsarmee" komponiert ist und mit ihr auch in einem inhaltlichen Zusammenhang steht, so werden Sie auch bemerken, dass jedes dieser "wissenschaftlichen" Kapitel mit dem vorangehenden und dem ihm nachfolgenden in einer Art kommentierenden Konnex gesetzt worden ist. Ebenso ist es mit der Stilfärbung, die im Huguenau wellenförmig auf- und abschwingt und dieser rationalen Wellenkämme unbedingt benötigt. Und als Letztes: diese rationale Sinngebung des Ganzen, zusammen mit den vielen rein dichterischen

Sinngebungen auf den anderen Schichten, schliesst es aus, dass das "Wissen-
schaftliche" als kristallener Block neben dem Roman steht; es entsteht vielmehr fortlaufend aus dem Roman selber -........ (53)

Has Broch succeeded in his aims? Hardly any other novelist can have set his
sights so high with a first novel; one can hardly fail to be impressed by the very
ambitiousness of his objectives. Even Broch, however, was not able to revolu-
tionise the novel form overnight. The problem of assimilation of the philosophical
content has not been finally solved: many readers will sympathise with Frank
Thiess, who suggested eliminating the chapters of the "Zerfall" from the novel
and placing the entire essay at the end -- as a commentary. However skilfully
Broch defends his composition, stressing the fact that the chapters of the "Zerfall" are in contrapuntal relationship to those of the Heilsarmee and to the preceding and succeding chapters, this is by no means always clear, at least to this
critic. Furthermore, the "Zerfall" seems strictly unnecessary, the philosophical
theme having been developed by strictly artistic methods in the body of the novel
proper. And these chapters of the "Zerfall" with their technical, philosophical
jargon, suddenly thrown in between purely novelistic sections, produce a jarring
effect. One cannot help thinking that Broch is guilty of that with which he reproach-
ed Huxley, Mann and Gide -- breaking off bits of an unassimilated "crystal block"
of philosophical truth to embellish the narrative, rather than integrating this truth
in the narrative.

And yet "Die Schlafwandler" remains an extremely impressive first novel. I
have already referred to Broch's astonishing virtuosity as shown in his mastery
of the many literary forms in "Huguenau". The various historical epoques are
brought to life in a remarkable way with their significant socio-historical diffe-
rences. One can not but agree with Broch when he writes, in a letter to his publisher
and friend Brody, apropos of a hostile critical article by Fechter: "Ausgesprochen
erbaulich ist aber nachgerade schon die Fontane-Walze, denn zu meiner Schande
muss ich beschwören, dass ich niemals Fontane gelesen habe; immerhin kann man
das Phänomen als Zeichen eines historischen Einfühlungsvermögens werten, das
Fechter eben bei mir so sehr vermisst" (54). This Einfühlungsvermögen, this
empathy of Broch, enabling him to penetrate into the very spirit of the various
epoques, is indeed one of the remarkable features of the trilogy. A vast social
panorama is made to live again for us through numerous characters of all classes,
religions and personalities, who are described in every aspect with such realism
and eye for detail, mannerisms and habits of speech that they seem to posess an
independent existence outside the novel, a truly Balzacian gallery of convincing,
flesh-and-blood characters. Nobody reading the "Schlafwandler" could doubt that
they are the work of a born novelist.

Broch has largely fulfilled his aim to transcend the naturalistic, psychological
novel. While psychological analysis plays its part in the trilogy it is only one level
in the complex, many-levelled structure of the whole. The main characters are
portrayed in the totality of their experience, from the physical and emotional levels
to the moral and metaphysical. Depths of consciousness are uncovered beyond
those of the Freudian scheme. In this alone the novel is unique, except perhaps
for the work of James Joyce. And yet, while the narrative soars to these heights
it never entirely leaves the ground, the here and now. We are made to feel the

solid reality of the three periods in their political, social and cultural aspects and of characters such as Esch, Pasenow and Huguenau. Moreover, the latter are by no means mere puppets manipulated by the author to illustrate his cultural-historical thesis. Broch's comments on the method of Frank Thiess, in a letter to the same, apply equally well to his own method: "man merkt nicht, wann das Flugzeug das Empirische der Erde verlässt, es ist plötzlich in der idealistischen Sphäre und plötzlich steht es wieder auf festem Erdgrund" (55).

3. "FILSMANN" AND "DIE UNBEKANNTE GROESSE"

Having completed "Die Schlafwandler" Broch quickly became disillusioned with his own creation. In a letter to Frank Thiess of 6th April, 1932 he writes, in a mood of post-natal depression:

> Aber nun will ich wirklich nicht mehr davon sprechen, weder von den Schlafwandlern, noch von dem, was mir an ihnen wichtig war - fast muss ich sagen "war", denn schon versinken sie mir ins Vergessen (1).

In the same letter he describes the novel as an experiment which cannot be repeated. First and formost he seems to have had doubts about the method chosen in the Schlafwandler:

> Vollkommen einig bin ich auch mit Ihnen, dass das additive Verfahren, das ich für den Huguenau gewählt habe - oder zu dem ich mich mit Rücksicht auf den Programmpunkt "Sachlichkeit" stilgemäss verpflichtet habe - nur eine rationale Annäherung an jene irrationale Gesamterkenntnis darstellt. Und wenn ich eine Fortsetzung des im Huguenau eingeschlagenen Weges sehe und hoffe, so liegt sie in der Verwandlung der Addition in eine richtige Synthese: eine Einheit von rationaler Erkenntnis, Epik, Lyrik und noch vieler anderer Elemente des Ausdrucks zu schaffen, eine Einheit, von der jeder Satz gewissermassen geschwängert sein soll. Ob eine derartige Synthese überhaupt durchführbar ist, oder ob sie notwendig zu einer Darstellungsform führt, wie sie Joyce (dem ja auch die Totalerkenntnis vorschwebt) für sich gefunden hat, wage ich heute noch nicht zu entscheiden. Aber ich muss Ihnen zustimmen: bloss das Irrationale, das Dichterische wirkt von Mensch zu Mensch, bloss dieses ist imstande, eine Seele zu öffnen, und deshalb ist auch hier der Boden für jene angestrebte hypothetische Synthese zu suchen (2).

Before Broch's next attempt to express this total knowledge, before the next great novel, "Der Versucher", we have two novel fragments -- "Filsmann" and "Die Unbekannte Grösse". Broch began work on the first chapters of Filsmann in March, 1932. His intention was to show the continuation of the process of decline of values depicted in "Die Schlafwandler" in the years prior to the Nazis' seizure of power. Soon, however, Broch was toying with the idea of giving the material dramatic expression. He became more and more enthusiastic about the idea of getting the play on the boards as fast as possible, partly because he considered it would provide valuable publicity for "Die Schlafwandler" and partly for pressing financial reasons (3). And so, in August 1932, the play -- "Die Entsühnung" -- was completed. It was not, however, contrary to Broch's expectations, to have its first production until March 1934 in the Zürcher Schauspielhaus, with the title "Denn sie wissen nicht was sie tun. " Broch considered that the simultaneous appearance of the Filsmann novel and the play would involve waiting until the next theatre season for the first production. There were, however, other, deeper reasons for Broch not completing the Filsmann novel.

In a letter to Willa Muir, 19th March, 1932, Broch seems to despair of the legitimacy of art in an age like ours:

Wir müssen uns ja darüber klar sein, dass die Zeit für den Schriftsteller
vorüber ist, weil die Zeit eben mit Kunst nichts mehr zu tun hat (s. Zerfall
der Werte) und man muss dieses Schicksal bejahen: lächerlich wäre es, es
zu beklagen. Die radikale Konsequenz, die Joyce daraus gezogen hat, nämlich seine absolute Esoterik, ist durchaus bewundernswert. .... Die
radikalste Konsequenz, die daraus zu ziehen wäre, über Joyce hinaus: überhaupt nicht mehr schreiben, auch keine Philosophie mehr schreiben, sondern
sich auf die Esoterik der Mathematik zurückzuziehen. Und im Grunde habe
ich die grösste Lust, dies zu tun (4).

March 1932 finds Broch deeply concerned and depressed by the turn politics are
taking in Germany. In the letter quoted from above he expresses the wish to move
to England, to escape the poison which is infecting Germany's political life. This
note becomes more and more insistant in the letters, and the anxiety behind such
remarks must have been a further contributory factor in his interrupted progress
with the novel. On the 1st July he writes to Edwin and Willa Muir:

Immer mehr wächst in mir die Ueberzeugung, dass der englische Schriftsteller noch eine soziale Mission zu erfüllen hat und damit Lebensberechtigung
hat, während in Deutschland -- und vielleicht ist es darin moderner? -- das
Künstlerische und Geistige jeden Boden verliert. Es ist eine furchtbare
Atmosphäre, und irgendwie trage ich mich unausgesetzt mit dem Gedanken
nach dem Westen, vielleicht sogar wirklich nach England zu übersiedeln (5).

In a letter of the 17th July we find the biting comment: "ich glaube, hoffe ....
dass das Buch (Die Schlafwandler) schliesslich mehr im Ausland als in Deutschland
gelesen werden wird. Die Deutschen werden ja wirklich nichts mehr lesen, höchstens
die Biographie Hitlers (6).
In a letter of 25th November, 1932, to Frau Brody, wife of his publisher, he
gives vent to his doubts in the aesthetic field. Poetry means gaining knowledge
through form. Poetry which does not gain new knowledge is valueless. New knowledge can, however, only be gained by new form. This in turn means alienating a
potential audience. This fear Broch sees as the reason why, in the last year, he
has experienced an increasingly strong wish to return to his scientific researches.
"Die Schlafwandler und das Drama sind erste Etappen auf dem Wege der irrationalen Erkenntnis, die eben Erkenntnis durch die Form ist, und ich fürchte mich
eigentlich vor der nächsten Etappe. Vielleicht fürchte ich mich auch vor dem weiter aufbrechenden Irrationalen als solchem ...." (7). Apart from this reason
there were other, more mundane reasons for shrinking back from artistic experi-
mentation. Broch was obliged to earn his living through writing, and the way he
saw before him would inevitably lead away from literary convention and therefore
saleability.
In a letter to Dr. Daniel Brody of 9th December, 1932, we hear that approxi-
mately a hundred pages are completed. This must refer to the first draft. In the
same letter, however, Broch is thinking again of abandonning the novel in favour
of a cultural-philosophical book on the lines of "Der Zerfall der Werte". Again
financial considerations figure prominently: Broch thinks that such a book, supple-
mented by some pictures, would be a better commercial proposition than another

novel. And, very significantly, he adds "irgendwie entspricht es meinem Ueber-
Ich, nunmehr -- ehe der nächste Roman erscheint -- ein philosophisches Buch
einzulegen, ein Allroundideal" (8). Broch is nothing if not an intellectual and
artistic allrounder and this wish is very typical of the man.

On the 7th February, 1933, in a letter to the Muirs he directly attributes
his inability to continue with his creative work (the Filsmann novel) to the anxiety
induced by outside events:

> der Zustand in Deutschland, der aber nur Exponent des Weltzustandes ist,
> bedrückt mich unsäglich und lähmt meine ganze Arbeitsfähigkeit. Ich bin an
> einem neuen Roman, mit dem ich angesichts der Weltsinnlosigkeit einfach
> nicht weiter komme (9).

On the 27th February he writes in a similar vein:

> Aber von meinem persönlichen Elend abgesehen, bin ich von dem Zustand
> der Welt (mit Deutschland angefangen) masslos bedrückt. Und es ist irgend-
> wie sinnlos, ja nahezu unstatthaft, in diese Welt hinein Romane oder Theater-
> stücke zu schreiben. Erinnern Sie sich, dass ich das gleiche schon in Wien
> gesagt habe! und damals war es noch nicht so arg! und was ich damals sagte,
> nämlich, dass es noch richtiger wäre, sich auf die Wissenschaft zurückzu-
> ziehen, erscheint mir heute plausibler als je, umsomehr als mich alles zur
> rein logisch-philosophischen Arbeit drängt (10).

In a letter to Frank Thiess, 23rd May, 1933, we again find Broch concerned at
the prospect of following his artistic daemon into esoteric ways which would result
in a gulf between the work and the potential audience, thus obstructing the primary
function of art: communication. But again Broch is tormented by the problem he
mentioned in the earlier letter to Willa Muir of 19th March, 1932, a problem which
was to come to figure at the very centre of Broch's life and work -- the problem
of the legitimacy of art in an epoch like our own:

> im Grunde genommen weiss ich überhaupt nicht -- ich schilderte Ihnen das
> ja schon einmal --, ob Dichten heute noch eine legitime Lebensäusserung
> ist, ob das, was man zu sagen hat, nicht auf ganz anderem Weg und viel
> lebendiger in die Zeit wirken müsste. Letzten Endes könnte man eigentlich
> nur mehr Bekenntnisse schreiben, ohne irgendeine Einkleidung und nur auf
> das Wesentliche bedacht. Denn alles, was geschieht -- das wird immer deut-
> licher und deutlicher --, ist ja ein Ringen um die neue Religiosität, und die-
> se ist wahrscheinlich auch das Einzige, was den Menschen jetzt wahrhaft
> interessiert, mag es auch danach aussehen, als wäre die Weltwirtschaft das
> einzig Interessante (11).

This theme is taken up also in the essay "Leben ohne platonische Idee", published
the 5th of August, 1932. Here a note of reserved optimism is maintained: "Es darf
nicht vergessen werden, dass die Philosophie nicht nur Nach- sondern auch Vor-
Religion ist und dass im Geistigen immer noch das Platonische und die Freiheit
gesiegt haben" (12).

In a letter to Daniel Brody, 15th November, 1933, we hear of new reasons for
neglecting the project. Fischer Verlag had suggested that before the "big novel"

(Filsmann) it might be a good idea to publish a smaller book, which would create a steady readership, thus facilitating reception of the Filsmann. Broch is full of misgivings,

> denn ich habe mich nun einmal in den Filsmann-Roman eingearbeitet, der Problemkreis ist mir innerlich von grösster Bedeutung, und es wäre mir eine ausgesprochene Qual, diese Arbeit zu verlassen, um, rein von äusserlichen Gründen diktiert, mich auf ein neues Thema und auf neue Probleme zu konzentrieren (13).

In a letter to Brody of the 30th December, 1933, we hear that work on the novel has again been put off, this time in favour of a lecture preparation. Now he is toying with the idea of using the Tierkreis stories as a prelude to the big novel, although he has doubts on the grounds of their esoteric nature. The "big novel" was never to be completed.

I should now like to turn my attention to the much more substantial and, to my mind, more interesting "Die Unbekannte Grösse". The novel-fragment "Die Unbekannte Grösse" from August, 1933, printed on the 17th September-7th October in the "Vossische Zeitung", marks a turning-point in Broch's philosophical attitude and points to the middle period of his works. The "unknown quantity" referred to in the title is thanatos, shadowing the work from beginning to end with its inexorable presence. The central event, in the fragment at any rate, -- for Broch indicates that a continuation would have brought into greater relief the other members of the Hieck family -- is the suicide of Otto, younger brother of the young mathematician Richard Hieck. This is in itself a deeply tragic event, and the fragment would seem on these grounds to belong to the period of the earlier works. However, the conception of death has changed perceptibly, having notably a more positive complexion. Thanatos is no longer shown in its tragic absurdity, but as inherently meaningful.

The fragment was the product of "a grandiose scheme that Broch outlined in a lengthy correspondence with Warner Brothers. Broch, like C. P. Snow more recently, tended to regard himself as a mediator between two cultures. He envisaged a series of six motion pictures that would familiarize the general public with the mind of the scientist in order to combat the anti-intellectualism of the times" (14). "Die Unbekannte Grösse" has as its hero Richard Hieck, an intellectual, one whose life is "rein auf Erkenntnis abgestellt" (15). It is, in other words, an "epistemological novel" much as "Die Schlafwandler" was. And yet Broch seems to have realized his formal error in the former work and now sees the danger of overloading his narrative with undigested non-poetic material:

> Der Roman eines intellektuellen, in diesem Fall eines wissenschaftlichen Menschen, besteht nicht darin, dass man das Material des von ihm bearbeiteten gelehrten Wissenschaftsgebietes vor dem Leser ausbreitet. Was Anspruch erhebt, Dichtung genannt zu werden, hat mit den einfachsten Grundtrieben der Seele zu tun, mit Geburt und Tod, mit Liebe und Natur und sozialer Verbundenheit, mit den Ursymbolen ihrer Ausdrucksformen, nicht aber mit wissenschaftlichem Material: der Roman des Mathematikers Richard Hieck hat sich sohin mit der Mathematik so weit zu beschäftigen, als sie zum Kristallisationspunkt jener seelischen Urkräfte geworden ist, m. a. W.

soweit sie in der Mechanik seelischen Geschehens selber Symbolwert besitzt und der Erkenntnisvorgang der Mathematik als Exponent der tieferen Seelendynamik dient (16).

The novel is an artistic expression of the same ideas, the same cultural-historical philosophy which was the basis of "Die Schlafwandler" and found expression in "Der Zerfall der Werte". The following passage, which explains the position of the modern intellectual such as Hieck, could indeed have slipped unnoticed into the earlier work:

Jedes reine Erkenntnisstreben zielt letzten Endes auf eine platonische Weltanschauung, also auf eine, in welcher die empirische Welt völlig vom erkennenden Ich bewältigt und aufgelöst wird. In Zeiten religiöser Hochblüte wird dieses Streben zum sozialen Phänomen, in ihnen besteht durch das Vorhandensein einer verbindlichen Kosmogonie eine Weltbewältigung weitestgehender Allgemeingültigkeit. Dagegen isolieren Zeiten religiösen Tiefstandes den Erkennenden, sie stellen ihn vor die Aufgabe, mit der Weltbewältigung allein fertig zu werden, sie haben die Gemeinschaft aufgehoben und das Religiöse in die mystische Einsamkeit der Seele verwiesen.
. . . .
Mit der Aufhebung des theologischen Gesamtorganons wird der intellektuelle, erkenntnissuchende Mensch auf die Einzelwissenschaften verwiesen, die mit zunehmender Wissenschaftlichkeit und Mathematisierung immer weniger Möglichkeiten für den vom Rationalen nicht zu bewältigenden Erkenntnisrest übriglassen: die Mathematik ist der Typus des rein auf sich selbst gestellten, tautologischen Wissensgebietes (17).

It seems fairly certain that Hieck is, to a certain extent, based on Broch himself. Many personal traits of the author have gone into the character of Hieck, according to Ernst Schönwiese (18). Apart from the career of mathematics and the psychological problems which they have in common, the physical description of Hieck could well be that of Broch:

Aber ungeachtet solch massiger Unbeholfenheit, ja geradezu ihr widersprechend, war der starkknochige Schädel vorn mit einem Gesicht versehen, an dessen Fettlosigkeit und Schärfe man erkennen konnte, dass es sich mit der Zeit -- entsprechenden Lebenswandel vorausgesetzt -- in die asketische Härte eines Antlitzes spanischer Prägnanz verwandeln würde (19).

Indeed, one involuntarily thinks of the photographs of Broch is later years when reading the last phrase, in particular of the fine portraits scattered through the Rhein-Verlag edition of the collected works.

The novel deals with Richard Hieck's search for total knowledge. He seeks this knowledge in the individual field of mathematics, a search condemned to failure. In this searching for total knowledge within the strict confines and limits of an isolated discipline, Hieck is a child of his times, a representative of the position of the modern intellectual as outlined by Broch in the passage quoted above. Hieck's choice of mathematics is partly a reaction against the obscurity and ambiguity of the father, who rejected reality, saying that "die Welt brennt in uns, nicht ausser uns", and was orientated toward the night-side of existence. Hieck's father never took his children for walks in the day time like other fathers. The only time this occurred was at night. He took Richard for a walk across fields, picking flowers on the way. He carried the flowers in his hand, leading Richard to assume they were for the house. Arriving at the bridge, however, he threw them into the river, observing "Sterne im Wasser". This phrase unites the two main groups of symbols used in the novel -- symbols of darkness and of light, the light of rational, scientific knowledge, and is taken up as a theme in various variations throughout the novel.

The irrational or emotive aspects of life are symbolised by the colour black, the rational, unambiguous aspects by white. Erna Magnus represents for Hieck a real woman, irrational, unpredictable, provocative, too full of life to stay in the academic orbit. When he meets her at the swimming pool she is wearing a black swimming costume. Ilse, on the other hand, whom he associates with the institute and his mathematical work (for which reason he sees her as somehow unfeminine), wears white. The night is another symbol of the non-rational side of life. Women are therefore seen as "Nachtmenschen" by Hieck. The symbols are combined in various ways, as is usual with Broch, although the symbolism in this fragment is rudimentary and undeveloped by his standards: "und der Nachthimmel leuchtete schwarz wie ein feuchter Badeanzug". The symbol of diamonds on a ground of black velvet suggests the integration of the two opposing aspects of life for which he strives. The night sky is another symbol of this integration of light and dark and explains Hieck's attraction to astronomy, although at this stage he tries to penetrate the irrational rationally, rather than to integrate the two.

Through Hieck's father the lives of the whole family take on a shadowy aspect, all relationships become ambiguous. When he died his death was hardly noticed, it was merely a difference of degree, an unreal death after an unreal life. The influence of this "night person" made itself felt on all members of the family, although it manifested itself in different ways. All are one-sided, unintegrated, either overly worldly like Emily or spiritually one-sided like Susanne or Hieck. With Rudolf it showed in a certain wildness and restlessness, as it did in the case of Emily, who, after a passionate but unhappy love affair, led the life of a play-girl in Berlin. Susanne was preparing to enter a nunnery, shunning the world like her father. Otto, the youngest, seemed, with his cheerful worldliness, to have nothing of his father's nocturnal nature, and yet he cannot escape his inheritance and commits suicide. Richard's choice of mathematics is a reaction against the ambiguity of his father's life, an attempt to find the clarity and security, the certainty denied him by his childhood. Hieck sees mathematics as the answer to his life's problems. He dreams of illuminating the dark, chaotic, irrational side of life by means of logical order in the form of mathematics. He hopes eventually that all the ambiguous, shadowy, irrational aspects of life will yield to the ordered, logical, unambiguous mathematical vision. The solution of the mathematical problems on which he is working at the institute and the solution of his personal problems are one in Hieck's mind. Hieck seeks to discover the key to eros, thanatos, and the ultimate questions of existence within the field of mathematics, hoping that a solution of the mathematical problems of infinity will provide the key to the problem of infinite life. Rather than integrate the dark forces, at this stage Hieck dreams of solving all ambiguities, of reducing all the inexplicable aspects of life to crystal-clear, logical relationships.

What more natural than that he should now choose astronomy as that field in which the deeper purpose of his mathematical studies might most fully be realized? Here again Hieck is rebelling against his father's predilection for the nocturnal side of existence, for astronomy is after all the penetration of "die Tiefe der nächtlichen Sphäre und ihr dunkles Licht" (20) by the bright clarity of knowledge.

Gradually Hieck realizes that mathematics is, for him, a substitute for something else. "Er wollte mit der Mathematik etwas erzwecken, etwas, das so ausserhalb der Mathematik lag wie Christus ausserhalb der ihm dienenden Kirche, doch er gelangte niemals über die internen mathematischen Zwecke hinaus" (21). Mathematics ceases to be his goal, in fact he has no clear goal anymore and envies his sister, Susanne, with her naive, traditional religiosity, which nevertheless gives her a metaphysical security denied to him.

Hieck begins to realize the futility of his attempts so far to gain absolute knowledge in the interview with Professor Weitprecht, which constitutes the philosophical core of the novel. Hieck sees in the figure of the aged mathematician, as if helf up in a mirror, an image of himself in forty years. Weitprecht is a graphic warning to him of the futility of the mathematical approach to the ultimate questions of existence.

Hieck finds the aged Weitprecht despondent. He feels that his life, spent in the pursuit of knowledge, has not been truly fulfilled. He feels, moreover, guilty for the wrong he has committed in the name of knowledge. He interprets his lack of success in the academic profession as a punishment for this wrong. For over the small problems of the academic daily round he has overlooked the great problems of human existence. For this man dedicated to the operations of the mind the inevitable decay of the body comes as a shock for which he is ill prepared. He realizes that, preoccupied as he has been with his search for knowledge, he has not come to terms with his own death, or with death as a metaphysical reality. Knowledge itself is holy, Weitprecht tells Hieck,

> doch es ist die Heiligkeit des Lebens, und der Tod wird darüber vergessen ..... hören Sie, die Heiligkeit des Todes ..... wer an der wissenschaftlichen Erkenntnis arbeitet, arbeitet mit siebzig genau so wie er mit dreissig gearbeitet hat ..... und schliesslich wird er gefällt, mittendrin gefällt, aber an keinem Ende, weil er seines eigenen Todes vergessen hat ..... ein böser Mensch mit einem bösen Herzen ..... (22)

If Hieck's first genuine experience of love showed him the futility of his previous attempts to gain absolute knowledge, real enlightenment comes only with the spiritual shock of his brother's death:

> vor dem Leichnam des Bruders wird ihm die ursprüngliche Erkenntnisquelle seines Seins sichtbar, und er erfasst, dass die rationale und wissenschaftliche Erkenntnis bloss einen Teil einer grösseren und zugleich einfältigeren Erkenntnis darstellt, einer wahrhaft mystischen Erkenntnis, die beweislos und doch evident ist, weil sie Leben und Tod, Rationales und Irrationales umschliesst (23).

The experience of death closes the circle of his incomplete knowledge and, paradoxically, in the moment of experiencing death Hieck has an intimation of what love really is. Eros and thanatos are seen as related. For the revelation afforded him by the experience of his brother's death is that of the mystical coincidentia oppositorum, which sees life and death, love and knowledge, body and mind, emotion and reason not as irreconcilable opposites, but as complementary. Richard reflects

Auch die Wissenschaft is heilig, auch sie trägt die Heiligkeit des Lebens ..... Doch die Heiligkeit des Todes ist die Liebe: erst Tod und Leben zusammen bilden die Ganzheit des Seins, und das Gesamterkennen ruht im Tode (24).

Richard has not merely been shaken to the depths of his being by personal grief at Otto's death, but has come to terms with thanatos, with death as a metaphysical reality. The knowledge gained in that flash of intuition reached beyond Otto's death to a grasping of the world's totality,

die einfältige und grosse Erkenntnis des Seins schlechthin, unabhängig von jedem Seinsinhalt, verbunden jeglichem Sein, ... allumfassend in ihrer Einfachheit und in der Einsamkeit des Gefühls, letzte Evidenz des Logischen ..... (25).

Like Kant's moral imperative this knowledge is apriori knowledge, knowledge of the heart, unprovable, "unscientific", and yet sublating both rational and irrational knowledge, valid without proof, existential, felt knowledge. The heart is seen as "eine Resultante in einem Kräfteparallelogramm zwischen oben und unten" (26). This knowledge is love, the knowledge of the heart, and love is nothing more or less than knowledge. Through her experience of love Ilse Nydhalm has a glimpse of a higher dimension of reality, inexpressable by either mathematical formulae or words, "eine erregende Transposition in eine Wirklichkeit zweiter Ordnung, die sich mit nichts mehr deckte und trotzdem die Evidenz vollkommener Wahrheit in sich trug" (27). It is the same experience Gladys has when listening to music in the "Filsmann" fragment:

Atmen der Musik! beschwörend flehte der Dirigent um grössere Töne, doch wenn er sie bekam, so beschwichtigte er sie allsogleich im Auf und Ab des erhabenen Seins. Atmen der Musik, Eindringen des Alls in den Menschen, Verwobenheit der atmenden Seele mit dem All. Schwingungen der Luft, dennoch Schwingung des Odems Gottes, vernehmlich selbst noch dem, der im Nichts erstarrt ist (28).

This insight of Hieck, Gladys and Ilse gives a glimpse of a higher, platonic order, and yet it is only a glimpse. A little light is shed on the uncertainty of the goal for Hieck and for all of us by implication. And yet full, total knowledge is still unattained. The question "Genügte das nicht?" in the last two pages raises doubts in our minds by its very repetition (four times) and restrains us from claiming too much for this insight, from premature optimism. Hieck is, in Broch's words, "einer der kleinen Kärrner, die an der Gestaltung der Zukunft mitarbeiten" (29).

Hieck's spiritual progress in this novel reminds one inevitably of Broch's own path from student of mathematics and positivist philosophy to novelist. Broch was lead to take up creative writing by the desire to find a mode of expression for the

kind of non-scientific knowledge of the world which Hieck experiences here. It
should not be thought, however, that Broch is suggesting that the scientific method,
as represented here by mathematics, is made redundant by this more irrational,
poetic knowledge. In his essay "Einheit wissenschaftlicher und dichterischer Erkenntnis", published on the 16th July, immediately before the novel, Broch defines
the limits of scientific and poetic knowledge. The task of poetry in its Goethean
sense is

> Fortsetzung der rationalen Erkenntnis über die rationale Grenze hinaus, ist
> Hinabsteigen ins Irrationale und zu den Müttern, und ebendiese Totalität
> des Erkennens und Erlebens, diese letzte Bewältigung des Chaotischen,
> dem Goetheschen Schaffen voranschwebend, sie gibt ihm jene Richtung, die
> zwar auf das Ziel aller Wissenschaft, nämlich auf die Erkenntnis an sich hin-
> weist, und trotz alledem nicht im Strombett der Wissenschaft liegt, sondern
> wie eine unterirdische mächtige Wasserader den Strom begleitet, immer wie-
> der emporbrechend, immer aufs neue ihn speisend (30).

The essence of the scientific method, on the other hand, is

> positivistisch, es ist dem Spekulativen und Theologischen abgekehrt, es will
> immerzu auf das Unmittelbare und Wirkliche rekurrieren (31).

The object of Broch's life and work, as it was with Goethe, is to synthesize these
two branches of knowledge, which are complementary, not mutually exclusive, to
achieve the synthesis of poetic and scientific knowledge which Goethe called "Bildung". It is highly significant that Broch should take Goethe as his starting point --
there can be few men of our times who have so successfully bridged the gap
between the "two cultures" as Broch. He comes nearer to the Goethean ideal of
Bildung than any other modern writer. It is Broch's belief, as it was Goethe's,
that scientific and artistic knowledge are branches of the same tree -- the tree
of knowledge.

One is tempted to dismiss "Die Unbekannte Grösse" as being inferior,
especially in the light of Broch's own comment to the effect that it was lightweight,
commercial and written in a hurry (three months) to satisfy the publisher and for
financial reasons (32). If Broch seems to place any value on the work it is in as
far as it is a preparation for the Filsmann novel. It is, of course, a fragment,
and much of the criticism one might make on literary grounds would be superfluous
in the light of this fact. One misses the involved counterpoint of symbols and
symbol-clusters typical of Broch; here the symbolism is rudimentary and clearly
undeveloped. The characterisation is rather perfunctory. And yet, having said
that, who can forget the tragi-comic figure of Weitprecht, comic in his scholarly
alienation from life and in his absent-mindedness, tragic in his failure both as a
scholar and as a man, a character as fully realized as any in Broch's work and
who lives in the memory as real as many people one knows in real life, in fact
more real than most.

If the fragment lacks the tautness of construction, the depth of characterisation
and the symbolic density we have come to expect from Broch, despite these literary
defects, which stem from the haste with which it was written, the work occupies an
important place in Broch's oeuvre. While the story is to a certain extent a further

variation on the "Schlafwandler" theme, it advances beyond the earlier work in terms of content and anticipates "Der Versucher", the major work in Broch's middle period. "Die Ideen- und Themenwelt des "Versuchers", "Vergil" und der "Schuldlosen" sind keimenhaft schon in der "Unbekannten Grösse" zu finden", remarks Ernst Schönwiese (33). Egon Vietta also appears to have recognised the distance covered since "Die Schlafwandler", in an article which appeared in the Neue Rundschau, 1934:

> die Einsamkeit des Nichtwissens wird vom Menschen nicht genommen . . . . . Gleichwohl schlägt er die Saiten einer hohen Offenbarung an, die in unge-zwungener Klarheit plötzlich den Menschen überkommen kann, als Gnade der platonischen Schau. . . . . . Es ist die erschreckende Gewissheit einer anderen Ordnung, die sich im menschlichen Sein nicht begreifen, kaum ahnen lässt . . . . . (34).

4. "DER VERSUCHER"

The text which we have in front of us in the Rhein Verlag edition of the collected works, called "Der Versucher", is the result of piecing together sections of the three different versions (two drafts written between 1934 and 1936 and a revision (1950-51). Felix Stössinger gives a reasoned defence of his procedural method in editing in his "Nachwort des Herausgebers" and I consider his reasons valid. Certainly the best tribute to his literary taste and understanding of Broch's work is the fact that the text reads like a completed Broch novel: nowhere do we feel a lack of unity, either stylistically or otherwise.

Originally the novel was planned as volume one of a religious trilogy, dealing with the primitive earth and mother cult (1). Indeed, Broch often referred to the novel as the "Demeter novel". Demeter was, in ancient times, a corn-deity with her seat at Eleusis, and in fact Demeter-worship continued after the advent of Christianity down until the nineteenth century, when Clarke took back the magnificent image of Demeter which is now to be found in the University of Cambridge. The rape of Persephone by Pluto, Lord of the Underworld, and the mourning of her mother Demeter is usually interpreted by anthropologists as relating to vegetation rituals, the ritualistic celebration of the sinking of seeds into the dark earth and the "resurrection" of the seed in the form of corn, in the spring. More recent anthropologists such as Radin, however, tend to modify this view of mythology in terms of nature-phenomena. Sir James Frazer himself, in his book "The Golden Bough", concedes that the Demeter myth has also a further dimension, a symbolic application to human life.

Stössinger considers the title "Demeter" mythologically untenable and considers Mutter Gisson to be an incorporation of the universal Great Mother, rather than Demeter. According to him only mythological allusions connect her with Demeter (2). Stössinger also points out that the physical mother/daughter relationship is lacking. While agreeing with Stössinger that Mutter Gisson is a modern Magna Mater I think it would be more accurate to say that there is some mythological confusion rather than that Broch did not have the Demeter myth in mind. Irmgard may not be literaly Mutter Gisson's daughter but the relationship is close enough and she certainly mourns her like a daughter when Mario, Lord of intellectual and spiritual darkness, takes her to the underworld of death. Agathe is her adopted daughter and in her child the resurrection element of the myth is carried. In the closing lines of the novel we are promised great things of Agathe's child, even the realisation of the new form of religion which the world awaits, the introduction of a new era. So one can see in broad outline the relatedness to the Demeter myth.

Having said this, I nevertheless prefer Stössinger's title "Der Versucher", for the mythology is certainly not presented for its own sake, but to illustrate the primitive elements in Man which the demagogue can revive and exploit for his own ends. The interest lies partly in the mystical vision of truth of Mutter Gisson (her surname is an anogram of gnosis) and partly, or even mainly in the depiction of the process whereby a demogogue turns a community into a pack of bloodthirsty,

heathen savages. It is the artistic treatment of Broch's masterly theoretical
analysis of mass-psychology. The mass-psychological theme lies at the heart of
the book and hence I think Stössinger's title places the stress in the right place.

Broch ceased work on the trilogy in 1936, having only completed volume one,
because the Vergil material was of greater importance to him (3). Also he was
disappointed with the progress, or rather lack thereof, made in the draft of
volume one, both concerning the exploration of non-rational truth and in its poetic
expression (4). Why should the Vergil material have proved more interesting to
him than that of "Der Versucher" at this time? The answer leads us straight to a
central preoccupation of Broch's, which was to become from now on almost an
obsession: the justification of the novel -- and other works of art for that matter --
in an age of nazism, gas chambers and other unprecedented horrors. In a letter to
Egon Vietta of the 21st September, 1935, Broch raises the key question whether
the profession of writer is legitimate in our day and age:

> hat der Lese-Ekel, der die heutige Welt erfasst hat, nicht seine tiefere
> (metaphysische) Berechtigung? Sie haben einmal ganz richtig angedeutet,
> dass es nicht angeht, den heutigen Weltzustand zu beklagen und anzuklagen;
> auch ich halte es für ethische Pflicht, "zeitgemäss" zu sein, worunter frei-
> lich nicht nur zu verstehen ist, dass man zu allem Ja und Amen sagt, wohl
> aber, dass man die nun einmal geprägten Formen akzeptiert und aus diesen
> heraus die ethischen Forderungen durchsetzt: wenn die Welt auf den Philo-
> sophen und Dichter nicht mehr hört, weil sie ihn nicht mehr hören kann,
> weil sie seine Sprache nicht mehr, sondern nur mehr die politische versteht,
> erscheint es mir beinahe unmoralisch, in einer solchen Welt ein denkerisches
> und dichterisches Leben führen zu wollen, denn es läuft auf eine Isolierung
> im Elfenbeinturm hinaus. Das Ethische und Religiöse in die Welt zu tragen,
> ist Aufgabe und bleibt Aufgabe; es ihr aber in einer fremden Sprache auf-
> zwingen zu wollen, wird nachgerade absurd. Gewiss kann man nicht von heute
> auf morgen sagen: "Ab heute bist Du ein politischer Mensch, weil die Welt
> politisiert ist", aber vielleicht ist die Schlichtheit eines stummen Lebens
> in solchen Zeitläuften richtiger und sogar beispielgebender als des papierenen.
> Ich habe mit diesem Problem unendlich viel zu tun gehabt, es war in den
> letzten Jahren eine furchtbare Arbeitshemmung ..... (5).

In November, 1935, we find him doubting the value of any non-scientific
intellectual activity, because the state of the world can not be altered in this manner (6). In February, 1936, we find Broch depressed at what he has seen of the
nazis in Munich and forming the conclusion that in a world where such things happen all poetic and intellectual activity is superfluous and outmoded (7). In March,
1936, one detects the same note: the world, in its present state of valuative and
cultural decline has no place for artistic or intellectual achievements (8). What is
necessary is some ethical action to alleviate the state of the world and the suffering
caused thereby. The primacy of the Ethical over the Aesthetic will be from now on
the guiding principle of Broch's life and work. In April we find Broch reiterating
his conception of the untimeliness of literature and literary problems in such an
epoque of horrors and giving this as a reason for not continuing work on his Joyce
essay (9). In November, 1936, he puts forward the view that authors such as Joyce

or Thomas Mann -- purely artistic writers -- are atavisms in an era such as the present which needs other things. Their work is seen as a pure luxury, totally irrelevant to the needs of the present (10).

In his essay "James Joyce und die Gegenwart" (1936) Broch raises the same question: "Doch wird damit nicht eben auch schon ersichtlich, dass in einer Epoche der Wertauflösung jegliche Kunst ihre Daseinsberechtigung verliert?" (11) He does, however, continue to furnish a justification for art, in particular literature:

> Mission einer totalitätserfassenden Erkenntnis, die über jeder empirischen oder sozialen Bedingtheit steht und für die es gleichgültig ist, ob der Mensch in einer feudalen, in einer bürgerlichen oder in einer proletarischen Zeit lebt, Pflicht der Dichtung zur Absolutheit der Erkenntnis schlechthin (12).

True literature shows an intellectual impatience,

> ein Vorauseilen vor der rationalen Erkenntnis, die bloss schrittweise und niemals sie erreichend zu solcher Totalität vordringt. Aber eben diese Totalität ist ja die Aufgabe der Kunst und der Dichtung, sie ist ja ihre Grundaufgabe schlechthin, und die Ungeduld der Erkenntnis, die sich gerade in der Dichtung ausdrückt, ist nicht nur die berechtigte Ungeduld des erdgebundenen Menschen, der den Tod vor sich sieht, sondern sie ist auch eine wahrhaft religiöse Ungeduld. Denn alles Religiöse greift nach der Totalität der Erkenntnis, alles Religiöse weiss von der Kürze der menschlichen Existenz und sucht diese kurze Existenz mit der Totalität der Erkenntnis zu erfüllen. Neben dem wahrhaft religiösen Menschen und neben dem Dichter steht immer der Tod, ein Mahner, das Leben mit letzterreichbarem Sinn zu erfüllen, auf dass es nicht umsonst gelebt sei. Wenn es eine Existenzberechtigung der Literatur gibt, eine Ueberzeitlichkeit des künstlerischen Schaffens, so liegt sie in solcher Totalität des Erkennens (13).

Literature, if it fulfils this highest aim, is valid even in times of cultural decadence when people may have little time for truth

> die Erkenntnis als solche ist nicht anzutasten, und die Erkenntnis ist es, die immer wieder, zumindest potentiell, in jeden Wertzerfall und Wertverfall, erscheine dieser noch so hoffnungslos, die Kraft zur Umbildung in neue Ordnungen legt, den Keim zu einer neuen religiösen Ordnung des Menschen, ... (14).

How are these statements to be reconciled with the repeated statements of the superfluity of literature? Broch thought that the 1934-1936 drafts did not fulfil this high aim of art and I feel this disappointment partly explains his abandonning the trilogy project. It was, in fact, a goal beyond the resources of his style at that time. In 1947 he wrote

> if art can or may exist further, it has to set itself the task of striving for the essential, of becoming a counterbalance to the hypertrophic calamity of the world. And imposing such a task on the arts, this epoch of disintegration imposes on them the style of old-age, the style of the essential, the style of the abstract (15).

Only in later years, with "Der Tod des Vergil" and the final version of "Der Versucher" did Broch's style attain final maturity, the abstractness and essentiality of the style of old age.

Partly also, while conceding intellectually, as in the Joyce essay, the justification of art, he saw that in a world of arrests, murder, rape immediate help was needed rather than philosophical truth. Brecht said that daily bread came first, then morality; Broch might have said that first came life, then truth. It was this sense of priorities which drove him to spend so much time, at the expense of his own work, helping refugees and people persecuted by the nazis in his years of exile. His complaints at having his work disturbed grew more and more frequent and despairing but, to the credit of this noble man, his sense of priorities never failed. I think it is in this sense that we must understand his repeated statements to the effect that literature is superfluous in an age like ours.

I think we are now in a better position to answer the question why Broch dropped the idea of a religious trilogy and left it at the draft of volume one, only completing it many years later in exile rather reluctantly, partly to satisfy his publishers with another novel and partly because he was anxious, very naturally, not to let two years' work be completely wasted. Apart from this the only other creative narrative work to come after Vergil was "Die Schuldlosen", written purely to satisfy his publisher. Vergil was the great swan song of Broch as a creative artist, the creative artist who was tortured by scepticism as to the value or relevance of art in an age of cultural decline. The fascination of the Vergil theme was that in Vergil's historical situation Broch saw a certain parallel to his own. But to this I shall return in a later chapter.

In "Autobiographie als Arbeitsprogramm" Broch writes of his aims in writing "Der Versucher":

> In den Jahren 1928-1935 veröffentlichte ich also meine Romane, ebenso ein Schauspiel, welches in Zürich 1935 aufgeführt wurde. Alle diese Arbeiten liegen in der Richtung, wie sie von den beiden angeführten Gründen vorgezeichnet gewesen war; sie bemühten sich um exoterische Wirkung mit Hilfe dichterischer Mittel. Insbesondere gilt dies für einen Roman "Verzauberung" ("Der Versucher"), der 1935 begonnen, aber infolge der Zeitereignisse nicht mehr völlig fertiggestellt wurde (das Manuskript konnte ich nach Amerika retten); in diesem Roman habe ich versucht, das deutsche Geschehen mit all seinen magischen und mystischen Hintergründen, mit seinen massenwahnartigen Trieben, mit seiner "nüchternen Blindheit und nüchternen Berauschtheit" in seinen Wurzeln aufzudecken, d. h. nicht abzukonterfeien, sondern es auf eine dichterisch einfachste Formel zu bringen, um solcherart das eigentlich Menschliche, wie es aus den Tiefen der Seele und ihrer Naturverbundenheit aufsteigt, zum Ausdruck zu bringen. Meine Hoffnung bei alldem war: die erzieherische Wirkung ethischer Dichtung (16).

The origins of the national socialist tragedy and such mass-hysterical happenings are shown via the story of the rise to power in a rural community of Marius, a dictator figure.

When Marius first arrives on the scene his appearance is rather unimpressive. His nose is sharply curved, he is unshaven, and his gallic moustache makes him look older than his thirty odd years. The surname Ratti indicates italian origin and this is also indicated by his curly hair; his whole appearance suggests a foreigner. One cannot help wondering if Broch is not here slyly alluding to Hitler's notably ungermanic appearance, which contrasted oddly with his racialist theories of nordic supremacy. His shoes are in a very poor state. Only the expression in his eyes and his way of walking are in any way remarkable; his gaze is dreamy and staring, but at the same time bold, his walk a strange mixture of austerity and elasticity. He gives an impression of stale, petty-bourgeois self-righteousness. His manner is compounded of obsequeous cajoling and doctrinaire presumptuousness.

Despite this rather unprepossessing exterior, however, when the narrator arrives at the village pub he finds that Marius has already made his presence felt with the chauffeur who gave him a lift. The latter pretends that he considers Marius' talk of chastity nonesense, but his older companion points out that he seemed convinced at the time of the truth of this doctrine, illustrating nicely Marius' ability to convert people to his way of thinking against their will or better judgement, as it were. Marius' words seem also to have made a deep impression on Gilbert Sabest.

The next glimpse of Marius is when he switches off the radio at the Wenters, under the pretext that such music is decadent and unsuitable for children and countrymen. He tries to impose his will on Irmgard and the others, "ein Schauspieler, ein Scharlatan, ein Hypnotiseur, ein Menschenfänger, einer von jenem Schlag, der Hass zu erzeugen trachtet, wissend, dass nicht nur die Liebe, sondern auch der Hass eine gute Bindung herstellt, wissend, dass man auch durch den Hass, den man erzeugt, Macht ausüben kann" (17).

Marius has an uncanny way of imposing his personality on people and great skill in manipulating them. After the fight in Sabest's pub he is the sole topic of conversation; whether the speakers are favorably or unfavorably inclined toward him the same note of respect is present, the same obsession with this captor of men.

He is very persuasive. When the aerial railway breaks, Marius interprets this in his usual fanciful manner: as heralding the advent of a new era. The mountain has brought it down. The earth is rebelling against machines and shaking them off. Although this is plainly ridiculous even the narrator is almost inclined to believe in this interpretation of the event.

He also has a very strong will, the will of a ruler. When Wenzel, his henchman, crosses him he deals with him summarily. He exercises tyrannical power over Irmgard.

His success in bringing people round to his way of thinking is explained in part by his ability to incorporate in himself abstract ideas. Partly, also, he supplies an answer to the despair of people like the Wenters, for whom belief in Marius is grasping at a last straw. Those who are the easiest prey of mass hysteria are those who, either by their own fault, or by the faults of the value-system of their environment, have lost their place in the system and consequently experience acute economic, social and spiritual insecurity. These people, faced with the spectre of a complete valuative vacuum, are thrown into a state of panic and the only answer to such panic is a substitute community, especially if a Führer, a leader-figure, points the way to such a pseudo-community (18).

The explanation of Marius' hold over people like Wenter is that their lives are so empty, so lonely, that they are ready to grasp at any straw. Often their marriages are unsuccessful, as in Wenter's case. Stössinger makes the interesting point that those who most actively support Marius are those who lack the all-important experience of love: "Der Verlust, die Trübung, Spaltung, Verwirrung oder Läuterung dieser Urbeziehung bricht oder stärkt die Ordnungskräfte im Menschen, so dass die Brüchigkeit seiner Liebesbeziehung ihn für die Störungen der gesellschaftlichen Ordnungen anfällig macht, ..." (19). Certainly love, as in most of Broch's works, is an important theme in the novel. While these people are particularly susceptible, due to their lack of love, to the pernicious doctrines of Marius, love-his love for Doctor Barbara-gives the narrator his first intimation of absolute reality, of the unity of all creation. Yet I feel that this particular point can be overstressed; it is but one factor in the process of bewitchment.

Of more importance in my view is the cultural-historical element familiar from "Die Schlafwandler". Marius gives an expression to the needs of people like Wenter which they could otherwise never find. He provides a kind of substitute for religion, a community which they are otherwise incapable of aspiring to. Wenter's succombing to the doctrines of Marius is born of despair: the old values of society are crumbling, the old beliefs no longer have a binding force. Wenter's world is that of the sleepwalkers, when one looks beyond the buccolic trappings. The dialogue reminds us also of the moral and intellectual bankruptcy of a people who were seduced by the master mass-psychologist, Hitler:

"Mag er ein Narr sein, mag es ein Irrsinn sein ..... wenn alle an den Irrsinn einmal glauben, dann wird der Irrsinn zur Vernunft ..... aber mit der alten Vernunft geht es eben nimmer weiter ..... und irgend etwas in uns muss eben Ja sagen, dann wird es schon von selber vernünftig" (20).

Marius gives expression to the thoughts of the inarticulate majority. The smith has, for example, a mystical conception of the mountain. For him the mountain contains truth and for him, as for most of the villagers, Marius expresses the thoughts and feelings which he, in his inarticulateness, cannot express. In other words he plays the role of the leader-figure, a role of central importance in every mass-psychological phenomenon. The autogenous forces in the mass, although recognisable as a general striving for values, are as such diffuse and directionless, and the more the panic increases the more directionless they become and an additional force from outside the mass is needed to focus the diffuse, autogenous forces on a definite, concrete goal. This direction-giving has the effect of a rationalisation for each member of the mass, even if it is carried out with irrational or symbolic means and usually under the direction of individuals who are more rational than the mass and therefore able to formulate the goals for the mass and to concentrate the diffuse impulses of the mass on these goals (21).

With what ideas does Marius fill their emptiness? His attitude toward established religion is one of contempt: he regards religion much as Marx did - as an opiate for the people, as a substitute for real knowledge. His own concept of knowledge is, however, wooly, to say the least. According to him knowledge is

"ebenso fest wie diese Erde" ..... "und es ist ebenso sichtbar wie die Erde und wie die Häuser und wie die Wolken ..." (22)

Like most of his outporings it is irrational, bombastically rhetorical and pseudo-mystical. And with its implied reverence for the earth (a veiled reference to the "Blut und Boden" cult maybe?) calculated to appeal to the peasants.

Marius' anti-clericalism is linked with anti-feminism. Hence he declares contemptuously that the church is a matter for women. The latter, according to him, want to prevent the dissemination of real knowledge. Anti-feminist, Marius is, perhaps understandably, also anti-sex. He maintains that all evil in the world is to be derived from sexuality.

He is also anti-semitic, like Hitler, on whom the portrait of Marius is to some extent based. He agitates the feelings of the community against Wetchy, not being content until Wetchy's house is destroyed and Wetchy and family forced to leave the area. It is interesting to note that the narrator is not immune to the mass-hysteria, and to observe his secret prejudice against Wetchy (23). Marius is the typical demagogue. As Broch sees it, the demagogue leads the masses along the path of irrationality, of the expression of drives in archaic and infantile forms of ecstasy; he appeals to the anxiety of people in a state of panic and tries to shape the forces of anxiety. Since, however, he knows that the individual is never inclined to look for the origin of the anxiety in himself but rather tries to project this outside and make some outsiders (like jews or negroes) responsible for the fear and anxiety, he invites them to physically anihilate these people. He uses with great virtuosity all the rational means at his disposal in order to create, or rather re-create, a state of affairs which human progress left behind itself long ago (24).

According to Broch's value-theory all things in the world which cannot be incorporated in the sphere of the ego by external or internal shaping are non-values antagonistic to the ego. A minority group within a community which preserves its cultural identity is, by this definition, a non-value for the community and potentially antagonistic. As long as the majority is in a secure position peaceful co-existence is not only feasible but a reality. But things are different when, as a consequence of economic, political or spiritual insecurity, the majority are thrown into a state of panic. Since the causes of panic are largely unknown they look around for a cause, and since the origin of the danger can only be located in the non-ego the outsider, the foreigner, is ideally suited for the role of the scapegoat. So, on one level, one can explain lynch acts, pogroms and witchhunts. But on a deeper level these are the products of magical, symbolic thinking -- the human sacrifice, with which the god is to be pacified. The Germans seem to be particularly susceptible to such atavistic reversion to primitive modes of thought and behaviour (25). But not only the Germans: every mass in a state of panic is subject to this desire for an ecstatic value-experience:

> Es liesse sich geradezu behaupten, dass im Massengeschehen die Sieges-ekstase - der "Siegesrausch" - beiläufig die nämliche Stelle einnimmt wie die Sexualekstase im Individualgeschehen, d.h. jene Stelle, von der aus das ständige Ekstasebedürfnis des Menschen am bequemsten, am handgreiflich-sten, also mit dem geringsten Aufwand von Sublimierungen zu befriedigen ist, allerdings zwar nicht immer real, dafür aber mit umso üppigerer Phantasie, und besonders dort, wo - wie bei Massen in Panik oder Vor-Pa-nik - der Wunsch nach einem rettenden Werterlebnis in Gestalt emotionaler

Superbefriedigungen auftaucht, müssen dieselben beinahe zwangsläufig . . . .
auf dem Wege der leichtest erlangbaren Ekstase gesucht werden. Sieg ist das
grosse Rettungssymbol, das den Massen vorschwebt, gleichwie die Fahne
ihrerseits Symbol dieses Symbols ist, und die Siegesverlockung war seit je-
her das Instrument gewesen, mit dem die Massen zu wahnhaften Handlungen
getrieben werden konnten: Lynchakte und Pogrome, obschon selber kaum
Siege zu nennen, sind symbolhafte Andeutungen von solchen, und sie sind es
umsomehr als jeder Sieg sich gegen einen "Feind", gegen einen "Fremden"
oder Fremdartigen zu richten hat, ja, umsomehr, als sich der Fremde,
möge er noch so harmlos sein, stets noch am geeignetsten erwiesen hat, zum
Sündenbock für eine Panik gemacht zu werden, deren Ursachen - dies gehört
zum Wesen der Panik - sonst nicht angebbar wären (26).

And finally he is, on principle, opposed to modern technology. He declares
mechanical threshing to be a sin. He seeks to support this statement by abstract
arguments which do not conform to any recognised logical rules, a somnambulistic
playing with reality, not influenced by reality but influencing it. He is, in fact, a
madman, i. e. one who lives, moves and has his being in a strictly subjective
"closed" system of values, which is not subjected to any checking against outside
reality. He is successful, nonetheless, because truth and reality are of little
importance to a mass in the throws of mass-hysteria. Victory is the main goal
of the direction-giving forces, as the above quotation shows, and especially where
panic is to be transformed into political energy by bringing together all drives of
the mass, however insane, it is the most effective goal. The panic - stricken
masses must regain their self - confidence, by identification with the leader or
leaders, who demand absolute trust. Since the mass think primarily in symbols,
the whole process is accompanied by very simple symbols. Fascist governments
have used their knowledge of these elements of the mass psyche to form political
conviction. This political conviction ignores truth and reality and believes only in
itself. Victory and success are its aims. A successful mass-psychosis becomes
irrefutable and can call itself the representative of the modern era. The direction-
giving forces, when transformed to conviction, take on a mystical irresistability (27).

From the above it is obvious that Marius' ideas are largely destructive. And
Marius is, in fact, a destructive force in a community: thanks to his own corruption
he is quick to uncover corruption in a society and, by uncovering it and encouraging
it, to destroy the society. His very presence is enough to make any organised community shaky and threadbare. He is an outsider, belonging to every community and
to no community.

What, if anything, does Marius have to contribute in the way of positive ideas?
He claims a mystical relationship to the mountain, maintaining that it calls him
when it needs him. He is given to making cryptic statements such as "seine Zeit
ist da" with an expression of empty obsession. With his divining rod he claims to
know when the time is ripe for mining gold in the mountain. While he exploits the
peasants' mercenary instincts in his talk of mining the mountain for gold, the gold,
for him, is merely a symbol of the wisdom buried in the earth, a symbol of hidden
truth.

Marius plays upon the ancient miners' superstitions, which are still very much
alive, and exploits them, incorporating them into his own mythology. In this mytho-

logy the mountain has the status of a deity. The earth, too, is holy. If man becomes unholy he offends the earth. This, he says, is the case with Kuppron. The mountain has been offended and will have its revenge, if it is not propitiated.

It may be difficult to imagine people being impressed by this kind of mumbo-jumbo but in Kuppron the mountain was already the focal point for a mass of folklore. Krimuss, for example, states that Death is to be found in the mountain, by the gold. Marius quickly confirms this. Krimuss pursues this line of thought, if such be the right word:

> "Wer das Gold herausholt, der holt auch den Tod ..... und ..... wenn wir
> ihn haben, den Tod, dann ..... dann erwürgen wir ihn ....." (28).

Suck relates a story of the remote past of the mountain, of how the dwarfs originally were in possession of the mountain (hence the name Zwergengruben given to the entrance behind the chapel) until the giants came, lured by the prospect of untold wealth. The king of the dwarfs offered them half the mine, in the hope that the two peoples might live in peace, but the giants chased off the dwarfs and killed their king. The giants, however, endeavoring to reach the gold, could not negotiate the narrow shafts and were either crushed by falling stones or drowned.

Pagan ceremonies such as the stone-blessing persist in this rural community, although they have been to some extent christianised. This ceremony originally consisted in the Bergbraut being walled in inside the mountain, or slain with an axe and left for the dragon so that it, pleased with the sacrifice, might let the mountain bear gold. Marius' revival of ancient mythology like this reminds one of the attempted revival by the nazis of ancient germanic religion. His success in reviving this mythology Broch explains by the revival of the heathen legacy in the mass mind, the re-awakening of primitive and daemonic instincts, which goes hand in hand with a deliberate loss of rationality (29).

According to Marius, who restores to this pagan ritual its original meaning, the earth cannot be propitiated

> "... bis der erstehen wird, der vom Vater Gesendete, der Sündenfreie, er
> selber der Vater, der das Opfer vollbringt, das freiwillige und schuldlose
> Opfer, rein im Blute der Jungfrau, aufgenommen von der dürstenden Erde,
> ja, dann wird die Jungfrau wieder zum Schosse der Erde, es wird die Mut-
> ter zur Tochter, Bitternis und Bösheit werden verschwinden in der Festig-
> keit der Berge, reich wird das Reine herabrinnen von den Triften, und das
> Meer wird die goldenen Ernten emportragen zur Sonne, goldene Spur des
> Löwen im Brote des Menschen, im Sonnensegen der Mutter, Samen der
> Sonne, Frucht des Vaters auf den Brüsten der Erde ..." (30).

And, furthermore, so hard is it for the individual to resist mass hysteria that the narrator is almost induced to take part in the dionysian dancing that precedes the ritual murder. The ritual murder is also preceded by some of Marius' most remarkable pseudo -- mythology, the essence of which is that the Bergbraut's blood must flow back into the earth in order that, by this sacrifice, the mother (earth) might be reunited with the father (heaven). The crowd scream for the sacrifice. Even the narrator, with his background of rationality and cool, scientific objectivity, is not immune to such mass-hysteria. Indeed, he cannot recall whether or not, in the intoxication, he joined in. In his "Massenpsychologie" Broch explains how it is possible for twentieth century people like this to be transformed into heathen savages:

> Der Mensch versteht das Leben, das er lebt, weit weniger durch die Wahrheiten, die er darüber hört, als durch die Wertrituale, in denen er sich bewegt, kurzum, die Rituale sind ein zumindest ebenso wichtiges Verständigungsmittel wie die gesprochene Sprache,
>
> ....
>
> Rituale sind sozusagen die Syntax der Symbolhandlungen (die Syntax der "Symbolvokabeln"), mit denen der Mensch sein Leben und seine Lebenswerte sich selber begreiflich zu machen versucht (31).

The mummers recommence their wild dance, shaking their percussion instruments, and everybody joins in. Suddenly Marius produces the primitive, pre-Christian dagger which he had found shortly after his arrival in the village. So carried away in the mass-hysteria and mass-intoxication is the narrator that he shares the crowd's disappointment at this primitive weapon and is full of understanding when somebody produces a more lethal, modern weapon.

As the crowd yell "do it, do it" a car's horn toots down below in the street, underlining the paradox of a civilisation which enjoys all the products of a highly developed technology and yet which has not advanced far ethically.

Secondly Marius provides a new sense of community for the villagers. His fascist view of the community or state seems to provide an answer to the problem of death, but it is a pseudo-solution:

> "Wenn alle beisammen sind, gibt's kein Sterben, jeder bleibt in allen anderen drin ... keiner lebt allein, nur alle zusammen leben, und deshalb kann auch keiner allein sterben ... solange alle zusammen leben, stirbt keiner allein; ein anderer tritt für ihn ein ... das ist die Unsterblichkeit" (32).

Inevitably one is reminded of the nazi slogan "der Einzelne ist nichts, das Volk ist alles."

At the moment, however, as Marius says in one of the Christ-like statements to which he is prone, society is evil and corrupt and "wo Unzucht herrscht, da gibt es keine Gerechtigkeit." He asks them to believe in him. The onus of regenerating society from its state of moral decadence Marius places on the young. When reading a passage like the following it is hard not to think of the Hitlerjugend:

> "Wenn wir Jungen bloss zusammenhalten, dann wird die Welt von uns bestimmt werden ... dann brauchen wir nichts mehr zu erbetteln, dann befehlen wir ... und wir werden dafür sorgen, dass es keine Ungerechtigkeit mehr gibt ..." (33).

In fact these "positive views", when examined, are far from such. His mysticism, centered on the mountain, is a deliberate attempt to conjure up the pagan past which is so near the surface of "civilised man". With his Bergmystik he has not understood Mutter Gisson's wisdom, that everything is a metaphor, an echo. His views on morality and society represent the "closed system" at its worst, for in as far as there is human progress it consists of an increasing knowledge of

inner and outer reality, i. e. it is an "open" value-system (34). Marius is a madman, and, like all madmen, thinks that he is the object of everybody's interest
and attention. And ultimately he is so dangerous because he is a nonentity, a
mere mask, who can offer men, thrown into panic by the valuative vacuum of our
time, nothing but a reflection of their own emptiness. In this he resembles all
fascist systems and all dictators:

> So sehr zugegeben werden muss, dass hinter den Kräften des Faschismus,
> oder richtiger aller Diktaturen sich das Streben nach neuer Werteinheitlich-
> keit verbirgt, mehr noch, dass dieser Uebereinstimmung mit dem "Gesetz
> psychischer Zyklen" wahrscheinlich ein Grossteil der Erfolge des Faschis-
> mus und seiner sonst schon längst gebrochenen Gewaltmethoden zuzuschrei-
> ben ist, es ist trotzdem kein eigentliches Wertziel vorhanden (ausser dem
> des nationalistischen Versklavungswillens), und aus dieser sehr tief sitzen-
> den Unstimmigkeit, aus diesem Streben nach einer chimärischen Wertein-
> heitlichkeit, die kein Wertziel, kein echtes Wertzentrum besitzt, ist es wohl
> zu erklären, dass die Faschismen ausserstande sind, den Bereich des Wahn-
> sinns und der wahnsinnsgeschwängerten Zerstörung zu verlassen, von innen
> heraus gezwungen, einen Wahn zu entfesseln, dessen Hypertrophie seit jeher
> Symptom eines zerfallenden, niemals eines werdenden Wertsystems gewesen
> ist; der Verfall siegt und hält sich darum selber für Aufbau (35).

We have described the role of Marius in the novel; now we turn our attention
to "das eigentlich Menschliche". The doctor, who narrates the events in "Der Versucher", has many traits familiar to us from earlier works. He is an intellectual,
for whom the pursuit of knowledge is the highest goal of human endeavour. Like
Weitprecht or Hieck he is dissatisfied with the strict limitations of empirical
science, "müde der Erkenntnis, sehnsüchtig nach Wissen". It is this dissatisfaction
with his scientific work, with the inadequacy of purely rational knowledge, which
drives him to the pastoral surroundings of Kuppron, surroundings which prove to
be more congenial to his spiritual aspirations:

> Diese ländliche Ordnung hat ein anderes Verhältnis zur Unendlichkeit als
> die städtische und wissenschaftliche, die ich nicht mehr ertrage und zu ge-
> ringem Bedauern hinter mir gelassen habe. Dort war das Unendliche für
> mich immer und ewig der unerreichbare Zielpunkt, hier ist es in sich be-
> schlossen, eingesenkt in jedes einzelne Element,
> . . . .
> Es ist eine Ordnung, die das Wissen der Seele und deren Unendlichkeit
> spiegelt (37).

The doctor was already advanced in years when he left the world of civilisation
and he himself interprets his flight to Kuppron as impatience for that final hour
in which the unity of all creation manifests itself (38). Indeed, the preoccupation
with death, not only as a physical fact but also as metaphysical reality, is closely
connected with the desire and compulsion, common to all Broch's characters, to
go beyond the boundaries of the Human, Temporal, Spatial. "Der Tod ist der
Uebergang des Lebens von einer Unendlichkeit in eine andere" (39). "War nicht

meine ganze Flucht aus der Stadt ein Versuch zu solcher Wiedergeburt gewesen?"
the narrator asks himself,

> war nicht meine Sehnsucht nach einem Wissen um die Ganzheit des Lebens,
> meine Sehnsucht nach dem Ausschreiten seiner äussersten Grenzen, war
> dies nicht ein solcher Versuch (40)?

Broch chooses a doctor for his hero for specific reasons. The doctor's whole
life and being is engaged in the Jacob-struggle with the angel of death. It was this
hope of overcoming the Dark Angel for all time which drove the narrator into the
medical profession, the hope that in thus conquering death one might overcome
one's own death (41). In fact the narrator sees the function of medical knowledge
"Zoll um Zoll den Herrschaftsbereich des Todes zu verkleinern" (42).

If the narrator has devoted his previous life to the pursuit of rational knowledge, in the cosmic harbouredness of Kuppron he learns another kind of knowledge, Pascal's "raison du coeur", "das gefühlte Wissen" of which Broch writes
in a letter to his publisher, Dr. Brody, 19th October, 1934 (42). This knowledge
is experienced in the centre of the human personality, "die Mitte des Herzens",
where diametrically opposed cosmic forces are found in harmonious equipoise. If
the doctor has previously considered death to be the absolute antithesis of life, in
Kuppron, under the influence of the environment, with its interrelation of human
and cosmic rhythmic cycles, and of Mutter Gisson's tutelage, he comes to see the
wisdom of the peasant's acceptance:

> der Tod ist viel, aber das Leben des Todes in der Menschenseele ist mehr,
> es ist das unerklärliche unablässige Werden des Lebens aus den Kräften
> des Todes, in der Tiefe der Seele, in der Tiefe des Berges, in der Tiefe
> des Meeres (44).

For everyone comes the moment when real knowledge is revealed, that final
moment when he realises that the life he has lived is smaller than real life. "Denn
zum wirklichen Leben gehört das Sterben, das sonst immer vergessen wird, ...
doch wem's aufgegangen ist, der nimmt den Tod zum Leben dazu, und nimmt das
ganze Leben zum Tod, ..." (45).
Such is the wisdom of Mutter Gisson, which the doctor accepts, realising the
inadequacy of his own scientific knowledge. Behind this conception of thanatos is
the mystical doctrine of the coincidentia oppositorum, central to Broch's work.
"Die Einheit von Tod und Leben trägt alle Gleichnisse der Brochschen Mystik" (46).
"Ich habe gelernt", Mutter Gisson tells the narrator,

> "dass wir in unseren Tod nicht hinüberzusterben brauchen, sondern hinüber-
> leben können und dass ein solcher Tod nicht umsonst und nutzlos ist, selber
> lebend wird dann der bittere Tod, und was lebend ist, ist niemals nutzlos.
> Ich habe gelernt, dass ich nicht zum Ende hinschauen soll, wenn ich es sehen
> will, sondern in die Mitte, und die ist da, wo das Herz ist ... ja, so stark ist
> die Mitte, dass sie über den Anfang und das Ende hinausreicht, dass sie hin-
> einreicht in das, was dunkel ist und was die Menschen fürchten, weil sie
> dort nichts sehen, als das Nichts und die Finsternis ... aber wenn die Mitte
> so gewachsen ist, dann wirft sie ihre Helligkeit bis über die Ränder und die
> äussersten Grenzen, dann ist kein Unterschied mehr zwischen dem, was ver-

gangen ist, und dem, was kommen wird, wir dürfen hinüberschauen zu ihnen, die gestorben sind, und mit ihnen reden, und sie leben mit uns" (47).

We might ask ourselves at this point what the exact nature of "die Mitte" is, since this concept is of such central importance. It is the same concept referred to by Broch later in the essay on psychology as "Ich-Kern", what Pascal means when he says that to leave the centre is to leave humanity behind-that innermost core of the human personality in which is distilled all that makes man human, "die sophrosynische Mitte zwischen Gott und Tier" (48). It is the Platonist's "soul", that part of consciousness which is timeless, beyond the streams of time which run through our bodily existence, the continuity of consciousness amid the manifold changes of man's earthly life. It is the "heart" in Pascal's sense, the divine spark which, by virtue of its divinity, is beyond the antinomies known to finite consciousness -- life and death, past and future. Beyond time, for it death, which exists only in the time-dimension, has no meaning. It is the divine spark by virtue of which is fulfilled the saying that God created man in his own image (49).

Wisdom Broch defines in the "Massenpsychologie" as "eher eine Funktion des Dahindämmerns denn eine der Erkenntnis; sie entsteht", he continues, "im Zusammenklang von Bewusstheit und Unbewusstheit, im Zusammenklang von Kultur und Natur ..... eingebettet in den Dämmerungsstrom, ein dahindämmerndes Erkennen, ein erkennendes Dämmern, Weisheit ist Diesseitsfrömmigkeit, und ihr Prüfstein ist ihre Akzeptierung des Todes" (50). Wisdom as thus defined is most clearly evidenced in the peasant. The peasant's fundamental sense of acceptance, which manifests itself in political conservatism, hostility to change, is founded on his organic relationship to the primaeval, cosmic rhythms of birth and decay in nature around him. Pious in his attitude toward life, the peasant accepts death with the same piety. The peasant does not concieve of the dead person as having another existence in a "beyond" but rather entertains the idea of the earthly continuance of the dead personality, the ancestor cult, which gives the dead individual his place in the chain of generations. Much as he accepts life in all its variability, the peasant accepts death as part of the rhythmic cycle of creation.

The distance separating "Der Versucher" from the early works is great. If no ray of hope was shed on the human predicament in "Die Schlafwandler" and the early works, if the castle was silent, sending no message to man, here the skies are still empty, the Götterferne is still unalleviated. However, Broch has found his way through to the mystical path of plunging down into the depths of one's own being, of ultimately finding God, for God is the depths. Mutter Gisson has overcome death within herself by finding through to the innermost shrine of being, beyond death, time and transitoriness, the eighth or ninth dimension, the dimension beyond dimensionality of which the narrator has an intimation. The search for God, the Noumenal, is also the search for the integration of the personality in the centre of equipoise, the

> Einheit, in der die Schau des eigenen Traumes zur Schau der Wirklichkeit wird, zur Ganzheit werdend und zum Ebenbilde, jeglicher Traumblindheit enthoben, Erfüllung der Sehnsucht, ersehnte Brüder meines Ich, und die ich doch nicht zu errufen vermag, weil jenes wahrhaft lebende, wahrhaft schauende Selbst so sehr in mich und in die tiefverschleierten geheimnis-

> vollen Gründe der Seele eingesenkt ist, dass es jenseits all der festen und
> wachsenden und wieder sich erhärtenden Schalen des Ich wie ein unberühr-
> barer Kern ruht, gefeit vor der Strömung, gefeit vor der Zeit, gefeit vor
> jeder Haltung und vor jeder Ueberzeugung, gefeit vor diesem ganzen Lebens-
> ablauf, hinabgelassen in den Ozean meines Jenseits, ... (51).

The difference between the earlier works and "Der Versucher" is one of
emphasis and degree, but not the less marked. If Man is still seen as a somnambulist in the vast dream-web which we call reality, death is seen as the moment
of truth when the true Sein behind the Schein of spatio-temporal phenomenality will
be revealed. Maybe this is God's dream in which we are all sleeping, life itself
"ein grosser gemeinsamer Traum aller Schlafenden". In the Demeter novel Broch
still places emphasis on the transience of physical existence. With the tortured
sensibility of a baroque artist he sees the skeleton in the living body. The media in
vita motif runs as a macabre bass through the whole work. The narrator watches
the peasants standing around, rooted as it were in the soil to which they owe their
livelihood, and to which their mortal remains must return, as the cosmic cycle
comes full turn, turned into wind, cloud and formlessness, "in jedem Anzug ein
nackter Mann, in jedem Mann eine nackte Seele". Later the narrator speaks of
"Der Knochenmann, der in all dem steckt, verpackt in Fett, Fleisch und Mus-
keln" (52).

The hideous, devastating aspect of death has been alleviated, however, in
the intermediary works by a newly found certainty of vision. Broch had been from
his early years a Platonist. But what had been intellectual dogma had now become
intense, immediate intuition, a grasping of that order behind the chaos of contingency, the Being behind the tawdry puppet-show of eternal Becoming, that
dimension of being beyond dimensionality, beyond birth, life and death, beyond the
alpha and omega of time-space existence, what was, is, and ever shall be, and
yet beyond the Was, the Is, the Shall be. Broch had been moving toward such a
standpoint in his epistemological studies, but the purely rational cognition was
superceded by the intellectual/emotional certainty of immediate experience. It is
an intuitive grasping of the totality of being such as is experienced in the remarkable passage describing the organ-playing at the church service, the ecstatic unity
of soul and world (53). It is the experience which Broch objectifies in the doctor's
intuitive grasping of nature's essence. It is a perception of

> einer Art Gleichgewichtserfassung des Seienden, die jedoch in Wahrheit jen-
> seits dieser Welt und ihrer drei Dimensionen vonstatten ging, losgelöst von
> allem Sinnlichen, Sichtbaren, Hörbaren, Tastbaren, und die dennoch, uner-
> reichbar vom Sinnlichen her, das treueste, täuschungsloseste, präziseste,
> unverrückbarste Abbild der Wirklichkeit lieferte, das Nächste wie das
> Fernste mit gleicher Kraft umfangend, eine innerlichste Schau und von ent-
> rücktester Ueberbewusstheit, die sowohl die Realität der unmittelbaren Um-
> gebung wie die der Seinsganzheit erschaffend durchdringt, durchdringend er-
> schafft, und in ihrer versinnlicht unsinnlichen Wirklichkeitsfindung wie eine
> Ur-Zeugung des Wissens ist, wie ein Abglanz des ersten Wissens, das die
> Schöpfung vollbrachte, Abglanz des Ur-Schreckens, der am Ur-Anfang und
> am Ur-Ende des unendlichen Schöpfungsaktes und seines unendlichen Wissens

steht, noch im Abglanz so heilig-schreckenserfüllt, dass wir solches Wissen kaum mehr Wissen zu nennen wagen, sondern nur mehr ein Ahnen es heissen wollen, selber ahnend, dass es das Wissen des Sterbenden ist, sein letztes und erstes, sein grösstes Wissen um das Leben, entlöst der sinnlichen Verbindung mit dem Aussen, das tiefe Weltenerahnen im Tode oder im Vortode, heilig sein Abglanz (54).

Death is now seen in a more positive light, as the moment of the soul's release from its bodily fetters, the moment of awakening from the somnambulist absurdity of life's dream, when the unity of all creation is finally revealed.

The novel concludes on a hopeful note suggested by the symbolism of the child: there is the suggestion that through Agathe's child might be realised the new form of religion which the world needs.

What of the novel as narrative art? As sheer narrative this is the most impressive of Broch's novels. "Der Tod des Vergil" is his greatest literary achievement, in my opinion, but can hardly be classed as a novel. "There is virtually no intrusion of speculative thought in "Der Versucher"; all the meaning has been assimilated into the action" (55). This is a great advance on "Die Schlafwandler", where the problem of assimilation of the philosophical content had not been solved satisfactorily.

What makes this novel memorable and remarkable, however, is the descriptions of nature, or perhaps one should say the overwhelming presence of nature. A new note is heard in Broch's work, a dazzling ray of sunshine brightens the all too familiar sombreness. It is as if Broch had read Nietzsche's appreciation and criticism of the Germanic mind and had learnt to dance with the spirit, overcoming the heaviness natural to the Germanic mind. Nature's spirit, like a tangy, invigorating spring wind, sweeps through the novel. Broch, who at his worst is turgid, pedantic, pretentious and unspeakably dull, is, in the finest of these descriptive passages, truly sublime.

Nature has been used before by Broch as a literary device, a symbolic backcloth for the action, particularly in "Die Schlafwandler". Occasionaly Broch uses nature in this way in "Der Versucher", as for example in the symbolic role of the thunderstorm, or the use of nature as a reflection of the human action when the narrator takes Rosa to Suck. The weather is used symbolically to an extent only paralleled in the work of Francois Mauriac. To say this is not to suggest that this is an artificial, contrived literary technique. Who more than Broch at this time of his life despised the merely literary? It rather reflects his belief in the essential unity of ego and cosmos. But the presence of nature in the novel is not restricted to such symbolic usage.

In 1935 Broch suffered heart trouble, immediately caused by an influenza epidemic but no doubt aggravated by overwork and stress. He decided to move to the mountains as part of his cure. With his new awareness of the Austrian countryside, afforded by his moving in 1935 from Vienna to the Tyrolese village of Mösern near Seefeld and later to the Styrian Alps around Alt Aussee, nature now takes on an altogether new significance. The perfume of clover fields and slowly mellowing hay spices the atmosphere of the novel with a pure sensuousness. The new relationship to nature was obviously of great importance to Broch, perhaps primarily be-

cause of the balance it afforded to his onesidedly intellectual life. In a letter to
Hermann Weigand he touches on this theme:

> nicht jedem, oder richtiger nur sehr wenigen gelingt es, sich das Leben so
> richtig einzurichten, wie Sie es getan haben. Als ich in den Tiroler Alpen
> lebte, ist es mir einigermassen geglückt, doch seitdem bin ich mehr und
> mehr in den Mumifizierungsprozess des blossen Schreibers geraten. Die
> Ausgewogenheit zwischen Natur- und Wissenschaftsarbeit, die Sie bewerk-
> stelligt haben, ist höchlich beneidenswert (56).

Fourteen years after his stay in the Austrian Alps we find him homesick in his
American exile for the mountain air:

> Ich habe das Gefühl, dass ich zehnmal besser arbeiten würde, wenn ich
> wieder einen richtigen Berg sehen könnte; oder genauer, es ist weniger das
> Visuelle, das diese Art Heimweh verursacht, es ist vor allem und ganz in-
> tensiv die Sehnsucht nach dem Alpengeruch, nach dem einer Bergwiese im
> Winter .... (57).

Broch shows himself to be a landscape artist of the calibre of Stifter. Yet his
is not conventional landscape art. "Wald- und Wiesenromane will und kann ich nicht
schreiben" (58). Indeed, he adds to Stifter's descriptive powers his own unique
ability to penetrate beneath the surface of space-time reality and show us the many
extra dimensions of Being. Rarely have the expressive boundaries of the German
language been so creatively extended. Indeed, the novel is only excelled in this
respect by Broch's magnum opus, "Vergil". Broch shows us the Infinite behind
the Finite in nature; in this not even Wordsworth in the great nature poems equals
him. Broch uses extreme realism, making us familiar with every inch of the landscape of Kuppron, so that we feel we know it like our own birthplace, but this
realism reaches a saturation point when the Being behind Appearance is revealed.
At this point the vividly real landscape, so vital, so sensuously present as to be
almost tangible, fades into another dimension where the Cosmic behind the Local,
the Abstract behind the Particular, the Spiritual behind the Material, the Infinite
behind the Finite is revealed. Broch's method is, in fact, a combination of extreme
realism and the transcendence of realism; Broch makes nature real, almost tangible, to the reader before saturation point is reached and realism is transcended.
This second layer of reality bears the same relation to ordinary reality as dream
to wakefulness:

> Ringsum sprenkelte die Sonne den Nadelteppich, das Bruchholz, die schüt-
> tern Grasflecken, die allüberall die Bäume dicht umsiedelnden grauen Zykla-
> menblätter, deren grünschwarze Zeichnung so sonderbar und doch harmlos
> an Reptilienleder erinnert, hartträumig der Boden, hartträumig die Stämme,
> an denen die Harztropfen klebten, sonnig in sich selber, freilich um bald zu
> weissen Streifen zu erstarren, hartträumig die schwarzverflochtenen hohen
> Kronen, tragend die Härte der hellblauen Ewigkeit, und das hartträumige
> Insektengesumm war vieltönig in die durchsichtige Wolke des Sommers ein-
> gesenkt, der Traum in den Traum, der Tag in den Tag, leuchtend und Seele
> in Seele. Einander träumend sind Mensch, Tier und Pflanze in den gleichen

Traum verflochten, doch wenn Trapp vom Nebengetier träumt, ist die Ge-
fahr der Jagdverflechtung nicht fern, und ihn an die Leine zu nehmen,
schien ratsam; also zusammengekoppelt, Träumende und Geträumte wir beide,
er mich ein wenig ziehend, wanderten wir weiter durch die vergoldete Starrheit, durch den abschüssigen Fichtentraum, dem Südwind, dem Hochsommer
entgegen.

Dann aber änderte sich der Traum. Nach und nach war das Gelände beinahe
eben geworden, der Bach breiter und langsamer, seine Ränder mit Stauden
und Gesträuch bestanden, und plötzlich ist er in einen von lichten Buchen und
Eschen umgrenzten Waldgarten, in einer kleinen Wiese ausgemündet, deren
leise Neigung so licht von ihm durchmurmelt wird, dass es wie ein Aufatmen
des Traumes ist, wie ein Umwenden im Schlaf zu sanfteren Träumen und zu
erlöstem Sein, umgeben von grünstrahlender Goldhelle, umgeben vom weichen
Säuseln des Laubes. Ueppig und voll und feucht ist das Gras, und in das Scharf-
blättrige des Waldes mischen sich bereits die zarten Aehren der Rispen- und
Flattergräser, sie allesamt überragt von den Glockenblumen, von den Dotter-
blumen, zwar auch sie noch der Waldflora angehörend -- prangend ihr Wald-
blau und ihr Waldgeld --, doch auch sie schon mit vielerlei anderem unter-
mischt; rosa und violett blühte die Schwarzwurz, weiss die üppig breiten
Schierlingsdolden, die ihr Frühlingsgrün zu verlieren begannen, und erstma-
lig in diesem Jahr sah ich nun hier das tiefe, unsäglich reine Blau des hoch-
stämmigen Enzians: Welt der Farben, Augengesang, letztes irdisches Glück
an der Grenze zwischen dem Diesseits und dem Jenseits, und dass ich darob
das in die Wiese mancherorts übergetretene Wasser vergass und einigemal
hineingeriet, hat das Glück nicht beeinträchtigt (58).

Broch excels at the seizing of those moments of transition between the seasons,
of those razor-edged moments where one cannot say where winter ends and spring
begins. The description on page nine is a good example: with a combination of well-
observed description and judicious metaphor Broch perfectly conveys the essence
of such a day between winter and spring, nature's balance being perfectly conveyed
by the artful balance of the sentence, content perfectly mirroring form. There is
a unique mixture of the realistic observation of one who really loves the countryside and is familiar with its every detail and mood and a highly artistic sensibility
which selects the suggestive detail evocative of spring's first stirrings:

unmerklich nur und leise bewegten sich die kleinen weissen Wolkenfetzen
mit dem oberen Wind von Süden nach Norden (60).

Equally skilfully Broch captures the transition from spring to summer:

Es dauerte wohl über zwei Wochen bis all die angesammelte Feuchte ver-
schwunden war, teils von der Sonne verdampft, teils in die Erdtiefe einge-
sickert. Zuerst wurden die südwärts gekehrten Wiesen und Hänge trocken,
dann erst folgte der Wald, dessen Wipfel spröder zu rauschen begannen,
ohne dass darum der Boden viel an Nässe verlor; nein, sie haftete noch
lange in allen Schattenwinkeln der Natur, und nach wie vor wasserreich
stürzten die Bäche den Tälern zu. Aber das Wolkenlose war darüber ge-
spannt, schattenlos immer weitere Räume des Aethers, und die Heumahd

hatte eingesetzt; überall hörte man es nun dengeln, und eines Nachts hob der Südwind an; frühmorgens hatte mich der grosse Duft, den er stossweise durch das Fenster trug, fast aufschrecken lassen, und ich erkannte den Hochsommer (61).

And equally skilfully Broch captures the essence of those November days when summer seems to be having a last fling before finally giving way to winter (p. 521). Often there is a new note of lyricism in these nature descriptions:

der Frühling ruhte im Himmelsgewölbe und eines Tags kam er zur Erde herab. Da zogen weisse Wolken, Schub um Schub, gegen Westen und gegen den Kuppron zu; sie verloren sich hinter dem Gebirge, wie um den kühlen blauen Himmelsraum für neue und wiederum neue Wolkenschübe freizumachen, und ihr Wehen, frühlingsgetragen, frühlingstragend, war das des wiedererstehenden Lebens. Es war nicht der explosive Frühling jener ersten Märztage, sondern ein haltbarer und richtiger, sanft und sachte unter einem heiterkühlen Wehen, und ebenso sanft, ebenso kühl rieselte die Himmelsbläue in die kreatürliche Welt, rieselte über die Körper der Menschen, und war sachte wie ein leiser Regen, dem man gerne die Kleider öffnen will. - So wurde es Ostern (62).

In his descriptions of summer this lyrical element rises to the level of the hymnic, the mythical. These passages read like an ecstatic panegyric to God, who is experienced in nature at its most magnificent, most vital and yet most spiritual. Who has so successfully captured in words the elusive essence of summer's magic?

Noch schwebte der Sommer, ein bewegtes Jenseits im Sonnenglanz, als wären die obern und untern Sphären noch nicht völlig einander verbunden; die Luft des Weltalls ist noch nicht zu jenem Glast geschmolzen, der -- wie alljährlich -- nun wohl bald herabsinken und den Wald ringsum erfüllen wird, die Stämme dicht umschliessend und in den Boden eindringend, gleich wie der Kristall des Winters es getan hat, traumartig wie dieser, dennoch irdischer, undurchsichtiger und den Gewittern hold: bindet der Winter stets aufs neue die Erde ins Weltall, es holt der Sommer den Weltenraum zur Erde, holt ihn zurück in den waldhölzern knisternden Traum, der vom Hauch unseres menschlichen Schlafes bewegt wird, obwohl die Bäche des Jenseits auch ihn still durchlaufen, so dass er uns selber wie ein Hauch durchläuft, ohne dass wir ablassen, ihn zu durchschreiten, als befänden wir uns in einem Wald, dessen Kronen und Wurzeln ununterscheidbar geworden sind, Mensch und Traum einander durchdringend, Nacht für Nacht, Tag für Tag, voneinander durchdrungen im Jenseits des Irdischen. Der Sommer nimmt uns die vielen Fragen ab, die wir an das Sein zu stellen pflegen; gewiss, er beantwortet sie uns nicht, aber er macht uns fragebereit, und mir wurde leicht zumut (63).

Broch's gift for seizing the elusive, subtle border situations of nature is paralleled by his gift for describing the more subtle feelings of the soul. Often the two are evidenced in the same passage, which is perhaps natural, since for the author nature and man are but echos of the same higher reality:

Ich fühlte mich jung, oder richtiger einfach alterslos, und mit meinen Beinen ausschreitend, wie ich schon als Kind ausgeschritten bin, wenn es galt, einen Berg zu erklimmen, atmend, so unbeschwert wie ich als Kind geatmet, das nämliche klopfende Herz in der Brust, das schon damals in mir geklopft hatte, wusste ich um die Zeitlosigkeit meines Ich, um die Zeitlosigkeit der Seele, unerfasslich die Zeit, die ich gelebt hatte, und der Tod, dem ich entgegenlebe, unabänderlich und doch so alterslos ihm zustrebend, dass mein Gesicht, unbeschadet aller Entschleierung, zu der es sich unter dem Befehl der Zeit hatte bequemen müssen, mir selber, da ich es bloss von innen sehe, nur noch verschleierter und rätselhafter geworden war ....
Der Schnee knirschte unter meinen Füssen; er ist voller Unebenheiten und voller kleiner Schatten, vom Mond, der hinter mir steht, ihm eingemalt. Da und dort waren die Häuser beleuchtet, und ebenso wie wir in Wenters Küche beieinander gesessen hatten, ebenso sassen in den Küchen und Stuben, von den gleichen nüchternen Glühbirnen bestrahlt, Menschen beieinander und sprachen von Menschen und Dingen, während aus unweigerlich städtischem, braunlackiertem Kasten allüberall die gleiche glattpoliert rasche Stimme bauchrednerhaft unbewegt die gleichen politischen Nachrichten verkündet. Allein, als ich aus dem Bereich des menschlich Wohnlichen hinaustrat ins Uebergrosse der freien schneeüberzogenen Landschaft, ins Menschen-Entflohene, Menschen-Entrückte, da ragte im Mondlicht mächtig und weiss die Kuppronwand vor mir auf, entrückt ihrer selbst, den Blick entrückend, so dass er, zarter und silberner die ferneren Gipfel, das Unermessliche umfasst und erfasst, den hingespannten Bogen des Gebirges, gelockert von den Nebeln des Nachthorizontes und in diesen verblassend. Mein Schatten glitt zweibeinig über den Schnee vor mir her, wies hauchend mir den leichten Weg, es wurde immer heller und es wurde so milde und strahlend, dass man vor lauter Glänzen kaum mehr die beleuchteten Fenster der Häuser von Ober-Kuppron wahrzunehmen vermochte: aufgelöst war das menschenhafte Sein im Unsagbaren (64).

One of the main themes of the book is the unity of all creation, of all opposites, in particular of ego and world. With consummate mastery Broch's style reflects this. So interrelated are ego and world that "alles, was die Natur sinnfällig dem Menschen zeigt, ist Gleichnis seines eigenen Lebens" (65). This is the key to the novel's ultimate meaning.

Broch shows his mastery of sensuous description and, incidentally, an almost Proustian gift for evoking childhood memories in their magic in the memorable description of the Kramladen (p. 110). But his real gift is for seizing in words the subtlest, deepest experience below the surface of the sensuous:

die Kuppronwand grüsste schneefrei ins Dorf herein, freundlich jeglichem Wanderer, und in der lichten Klarheit - die Almhütte am Kamm oberhalb der grossen Wiese war deutlich wahrnehmbar - schien die Welt zu wachsen, vielleicht sogar über sich selbst hinaus und ins Ueberirdische zu wachsen, denn an dem Wachsen teilnehmend oder gar um ihm Raum zu geben, hatte sich der Himmel zu einer höhern Farblosigkeit, zu einem höhern Schweigen zurückgezogen; das Sein war in eine zarteste Bewegung geraten, der sich der

Wanderer bloss hinzugeben brauchte, gleichsam als einer, der gewandert
wird, kaum mehr selber wandernd, doch als nun die vier Schläge der Turm-
uhr erschollen und ihren verzitternden Klang in das vielbewegte Wachsen und
Emporstreben des Frühlings verwoben, da wusste ich um mein eigenes Spät-
sein, in dem es für mich keine Wanderzeit mehr geben wird, sondern nur mehr
den ruhigen Weg des Alterns; es war eine schmerzlose Erkenntnis (66).

Comparing Broch's style with that of Kafka and Musil, Joseph Strelka finds
that it is to a certain extent a synthesis of the expressionism of the former and
the realism of the latter. He also finds a growing abstractness in the later works:
"es tritt -- besonders in den späteren, hier vor allem behandelten Romanen, "Der
Tod des Vergil", "Die Schuldlosen", "Der Versucher" -- das hintergründig Ab-
strakte, eigentlich Gemeinte, Allgemeingültige und Symbolische so deutlich zutage,
dass es sich als wesentlichste Erscheinung unübersehbar aufdrängt" (67) Broch
himself was conscious of a growing abstractness in his style:

Ich möchte jetzt noch hinzufügen, dass jede "reife" Kunst abstrakt wird,
dass sie sich bemüht, nicht mehr das Lächeln des Herrn Schulze, nicht
mehr das Sonnenlicht über Pötzleinsdorf, sondern "das" Lächeln schlechthin, "das" Sonnenlicht schlechthin zu zeigen (68).

Speaking of the nature of mature art Broch writes:

The "style of old-age" is not always a product of the years; it is a gift
implanted along with his other gifts in the artist, ripening, it may be, with
time, often blossoming before its season under the foreshadow of death,
or unfolding of itself even before the approach of age or death: it is the
reaching of a new level of expression, such as the old Titian's discovery of
the all-penetrating light which dissolves the human flesh and the human soul
to a higher unity; or such as the finding by Rembrandt and Goya, both at
the height of their manhood, of the metaphysical surface which underlies
the visible in man and thing, and which nevertheless can be painted; or such
as the "Art of the Fugue" which Bach in his old age dictated without having
a concrete instrument in mind, because what he had to express was either
beneath or beyond the audible surface of music; or such as the last quartets
of Beethoven, in which he -- only then in his fifties but already near to
death -- found the way from earthly music to the music of the infinite; or
such as Goethe's last writings, the final scenes of "Faust" for instance,
where the language discloses its own mysteries and, therefore, those of all
existence (69).

Broch is here discussing the mature style, marked by growing abstraction, of
other great artists; he might, however, have been characterising his own mature
style in "Der Versucher". It is equally the attainment of a new level of expression,
an artistic realisation of the metaphysical depths behind the visible in man and
thing, especially nature. Broch's style is in fact neo-symbolist, revealing the
infinite in the finite. Often Broch fails in this attempt to express the ineffable,
but sometimes, at his sublime best, he suggests it in a simile of visionary power:

"Wie eine Rose ist der Tag, wie eine, die immer weiter aufblüht und zum Himmel wird" (70).

How simple. How sublime.

5. "DER TOD DES VERGIL"

The short story "Die Heimkehr des Vergil" (1936) represents Broch's first coming to terms with the Vergil material. The Wiener Rundfunk, in 1935, requested Broch to read a selection of his poems as an introduction to their Easter celebrations. Broch, however, with characteristic modesty, thought that a reading of this kind would prove boring for a radio audience and suggested to Dr. Nüchtern, the director, that he should lecture on literature in a time of cultural decline. The tidy-minded Dr. Nüchtern declined, as this would have had to be classified under the scientific programmes division, thus causing clerical difficulties. Broch suggested a compromise: he agreed to write a short story on the same theme. The short story we now know as "Die Heimkehr des Vergil".

The major themes of the later work are already present -- thanatos, eros/agape, the socio-ethical responsibility of art, the futility of the merely aesthetic, Kulturtod and the messianic hope of rebirth, but lacking, of course, in the development in the horizontal and vertical axes which they received in the later novel. The long dialogues with Augustus, the interior monologues revolving around Plotia, which carry and deepen the theme of agape, the apparition of death in the form of the boy Lysanias, are lacking in the Urvergil, which we prefer to see, from the point of view both of form and content, as a fragment, rather than a rounded work of art in its own right. It is, as it were, a first draft of the Vergil. All that remained for Broch to do was to expand and develop the basic plan, to extend and deepen the basic leitmotifs, to shape the major themes into the grandiose structure with its four symphonic "movements" which marks the formal, artistic consummateness of "Der Tod des Vergil".

As a last point I would point out the preponderence of the thanatos motif even in the early fragment, although the particular symbolism connected with the Orphic myth is absent.

The genesis of "Der Tod des Vergil" was, then, a projected work on poetry in an age of decadence. Broch saw Vergil's age, the age of classical decadence, as an historical parallel to our own age. Vergil was a pre-Christian, one of those "who are necessary in order that the prophet shall appear, ... He was a pre-prophet, ..." (1). To minds tormented with the same sense of the problematic nature of life which pervades Vergil's poetry "the ideas that came from Galilee brought the rest and peace which they could not find elsewhere" (2). St.-Beuve writes "La venue même du Christ n'a rien qui étonne quand on a lu Virgile". At this time of cultural decadence the death-centred Orphic, Eleusian and Pythagorean mysteries, of oriental origin, took hold on the public imagination and found expression in Vergil's poetry. "The ideas of reward and punishment after death stamped themselves upon the common mind" (3). Broch, however, chose to emphasise rather the gap which separated Vergil from his contempories. Writing to Aldous Huxley who, in a letter of April 10th 1945, had ventured to criticise the "Tod des Vergil" on this point of historical accuracy. Broch observes that "Even though Augustus and his other friends ..... were in possession of the intellectual wealth of their time, the prophetic or pre-prophetic divination was not given to any of them" (4).

Broch thus emphasises Vergil's spiritual significance rather than his literary importance. The Vergil who became almost an unofficial saint, with whom even the Church had to reckon, is the Vergil emphasised here, the bearer of enlightenment. The chief requisite for this Broch sees as "a prior submission to "Zerknirschung" and self-extinction, embracing the whole life, and as I portray him as undergoing this ordeal, in a Christian sense he became worthy of grace, even though he actually never received it, since he had never been baptised" (5). Preparation for what is to come is Vergil's sole comfort in his despair and scepticism about the worth of his art.

It seems that originally Broch was interested mainly in the legend of Vergil's wish to burn the Aeneid (6), which suggested a parallel with his own doubts as to the value of art, indeed the ethical justification of art in an age of mass pain and terror, culminating in his turning away from the novel-form in favour of his sociological studies. In Vergil's desire to destroy the Aeneid Broch saw a comparable renunciation. It hardly needs saying that this renunciation is not born of any sense of despair at personal artistic inadequacy but is rather a spiritual metanoia, a rejection of sterile aestheticism, the "establishing anew of the verites fondamentales in the human soul" (7) which Broch singles out as the main theme of the novel. The dying Vergil is afforded a glance behind the curtain, as it were, that enlightenment "in which eternity is perceived within the things of time and nirvana and samsara are apprehended as ultimately the same" (8).

Much of the "Vergil" was written when Broch was really threatened with death -- at the hands of the Nazis. From this moment he wrote the book as a personal preparation for death, so to speak. It was an attempt, by means of extreme concentration, to come as near as possible to the actual experience of death without actually losing consciousness. In this trance-like state Broch wrote "automatically" the long, litany-like sentences as they came to him. "My task", he writes, "was to transmit to the reader perception as it came to me. I had to let the reader re-experience how a person draws near to the knowledge of death" (9). From the foregoing it will be clear to what extent "Der Tod des Vergil" is autobiographical. Writing of the novel Broch observes

Nicht nur also, dass der seines Sterbens bewusste Vergil zur Auseinandersetzung mit dem Phänomen des Todes gedrängt ist, dass auch die ganze mystische Haltung des Zeitalters, deren er sich -- verstärkt durch die Luzidität des Fieberkranken -- bewusst wird, solcherart zum Ausdruck kommt, nicht nur dass Vergil seine eigene Dichtung als Todeserkenntnis legitimiert sieht, es legitimiert sich als solche nun auch das Brochsche Werk: nur wenige Werke der Weltliteratur haben es gewagt, sich -- wohlgemerkt mit rein dichterischen Mitteln -- so nahe an das Todesphänomen heranzupirschen, wie es dieses tut (10).

"Das Problem der Todeserkenntnis und Todesüberwindung steht im Mittelpunkt des Romans", observes Strelka, "und damit auch eine weitverzweigte Todessymbolik. Auch dies reicht bis ins Sprachliche und wirkt stilbestimmend" (11). The first strand in this web of symbols relating to death is Vergil's crossing of the sea and landing at Brundisium, with which the book opens. The crossing of the sea, or indeed any journey, is an archetypal symbol of death and recalls the function of

Charon in the Aeneid. We are further familiar with the baroque symbol of the
harbour and the ship of life -- ultimately the ship of death -- from "Die Schlafwandler". Indeed, for a philosophical idealist such as Broch, the ebb and flow of
the sea's depths necessarily suggested itself as a symbolic representation of the
flux of life itself, fluctuating between Being and Nothingness, Life and Death,
"ein Strom fluktuierender Erlebnisatome, ein Strom, 'von dem wir bloss wissen,
dass er in den Tod mündet' "(12). Broch's prose in its tidal flow, its cosmic
rhythms, attempts to contain precisely this dialectical process, the constant flow
of reality. Vergil sees his own fate as analogous to that of the ship:

> Bild sich selber .... hinsteuernd zu wirklichster Wirklichkeit, getragen
> von unsichtbaren Wogen, eintauchend in sie, war das Bild des Schiffes sein
> eigenes Bild, aus der Dunkelheit kommend, in die Dunkelheit ziehend, in die
> Dunkelheit sinkend, ... (13).

On arrival at Brundisium Vergil is a dying man. The mark of mortality is on
his brow (14). He is a sick man overtaken already by the sickly-sweet odour of
physical decay. His physical state is emphasised by the decomposition and death
around him, making up the sordid atmosphere of Brundisium, holding up a mirror
to the dying poet:

> das schwerflüssige glatte Element, sich selbst ausatmend, Unrat ausatmend,
> Abfälle und Gemüseblätter und verfaulte Melonen, alles was da unten herum-
> suppte, schlaffe Wellen eines schweren süsslichen Todeshauches, Wellen
> eines verfaulenden Lebens, des einzigen, das zwischen den Steinen bestehen
> kann, lebend nur noch in der Hoffnung auf die Wiedergeburt aus seiner Ver-
> wesung (15).

Like Thomas Mann's Venice, Brundisium seems to conceal decay under every
paving stone, death in every cranny. The heady bouquet of mortality is insidious
in the very midst of life itself, as the life-affirming Roman populace prepare for
the Imperial festival.

Proceeding further, Vergil is carried through the malodorous, crudely
materialistic and obscenely jesting populace. The odour of these "Menschentiere"
is succeeded by that of the fish-market, "voll von Gärungshauch, ununterscheidbar geworden der Duft der rötlichen Trauben, der wachsgelben Plaumen, der gol-
denen Aepfel, der unterirdisch schwarzen Feigen, vermengt und ununterscheidbar
geworden vor gemeinsamer Verwesung" (16). In this twilight town life and death
are inextricably intertwined, two interlocking circles as it were, balanced on a
knife-edge, "des Lebens Ein- und Ausgang verwoben zu engster Verschwisterung"
(17), as indeed every second of life is balanced on a razor's edge, containing both
birth and death. If Vergil previously despised the filthy, vulgar crowd through
which he is forced to pass, in this moment of accentuated consciousness of his own
physical decrepitude and mortality love of suffering humanity flowers, a delicate
orchid in the dung-heap of Brundisium. The sight of some mistreated slaves moves
him profoundly. He will later give his own slaves their freedom as part of his
testament.

Here a second theme is introduced, political or sociological, of the greatest
importance to Broch, one to which he devoted much time and thought in the later

years as he became, like Vergil, disillusioned with art, and in particular the novel.
And yet, if it was the later years which produced the great works on mass psychology and politics, the theme is nevertheless one present in the "Schlafwandler" -
the problem of the modern mass. In this point also Broch saw a parallel between
Vergil's age and his own. The Roman Volk is seen as similar to the modern mass.
The depiction of the Roman mass is illustrative of Broch's mass-psychological
theories:

Ringsumher waren die Gesichter, Kopf an Kopf, Alltagsgesichter mit ihrer
alltäglichen, freilich auch schon weitaus übersteigerten Sauf- und Fresslust,
und diese Uebersteigerung, sich selber übersteigend, war zu einer geradezu
jenseitigen Inbrunst geworden, zu einem brutalen Jenseits, das jedweden All-
tag weltenferne hinter sich gelassen hatte und nichts anderes mehr kannte als
das Sekunden-Jetzt des übermächtigen, des leuchtenden Zieles, inbrünstig er-
sehnt, inbrünstig begehrt, inbrünstig gefordert, auf dass dieses Jetzt den
Kreis ihres ganzen Lebens beschatte und zur Teilhaberschaft bringe, zur
Teilhaberschaft an der Macht, an der Vergottung, an der Freiheitsgrösse,
an der Unendlichkeit des Einen, der dort im Palaste sass. Ruckweise, wellen-
artig, zuckend, angestrengt, explosiv, keuchend und stöhnend bewegte sich
das Gefüge vorwärts, gewissermassen gegen einen elastischen Widerstand
vorstossend, der unzweifelhaft vorhanden war, da er sich in ebenso ruck-
artigen Gegenwellen äusserte, und in diesem gewaltig-gewaltsamen Vor und
Zurück wurden allenthalben die Schreie der Strauchelnden, der Niederge-
tretenen, der Verletzten, vielleicht sogar die von Sterbenden vernehmbar,
mitleidlos unbeachtet oder gar verspottet, immer wieder jedoch übertönt von
den jubelnden Heilrufen, erstickt von dem wütenden Getöse, zerfetzt vom
Geprassel der Feuer. Ein ungeheuerliches Jetzt stand auf dem Spiele, ein
unendlich vervielfachtes, ein Herdenjetzt, aufgeworfen vom Gebrüll der Her-
den, ein ins Getöse gestürztes Jetzt und zugleich herausgestürzt aus dem
Getöse, aufgeworfen von Sinnesverwirrten, von Sinnesverlorenen, von Irr-
sinnigen, sinnesentblösst aus Seelenverlust, dennoch so sinnübersteigert in
der Gesamtheit, dass alles Vergangene und alles Zukünftige darein verschlun-
gen war, das Tosen aller Erinnerungstiefen in sich aufnehmend, die fernste
Vergangenheit und die fernste Zukunft in seinem Brausen bergend (18)!

The fruits of Broch's research into mass psychology are seen in the following
passage also:

So und nicht anders sieht die Freiheit der Volksmassen aus, und wahrlich,
sie wissen selber darum! Sie wissen um die tiefe Unsicherheit, in der sie
leiblich wie seelisch leben, sie wissen und sie wissen trotzdem nicht, dass
eine neue Wirklichkeit sie umgibt, die sie weder zu erfassen noch zu leiten
vermögen; sie wissen bloss, dass sie unberechenbaren Gewalten ausgeliefert
sind, Gewalten von unerahnbarer Ausdehnung, Gewalten, die sie zwar manchmal benennen können, als Hungersnot oder als Seuche, als afrikanische Fehl-
ernte oder als Barbareneinbruch, die ihnen aber, bei alledem, doch nur Ausdruck einer dahinterstehenden, noch tieferen, noch unberechenbareren, noch
unerahnbareren Bedrohung sind; wahrlich, die Massen wissen um die Gefah-
ren ihrer eigenen Freiheit, sie wissen um die Scheinfreiheit, die sie zur furcht-
sam aufgescheuchten, führerlos umherirrenden Herde macht (19).

Broch's analysis of modern man (20) is profoundly original and as valid today as the day he wrote it. Often Broch's sociological writings find an echo in "Vergil" (21).

Vergil feels horror at the other side of the coin of Roman imperial greatness -- the slaves, treated like dogs, humiliated, deprived of all humanity, bent double under their loads, thrashed without reason by the overseer. Surely Broch had in mind more modern fascist states with their scant regard and respect for human dignity. A close parallel to Broch's political writings is to be found in the following passage:

> "Magst du auch, o Cäsar, heute noch die Grenzen des Staates schützen müssen, grenzenlos wird das Reich sein; magst du dich heute auch noch genötigt fühlen, das grössere vom kleineren Rechte zu scheiden, unteilbar wird die Gerechtigkeit werden, verletzlich die Gesamtheit in jedem Einzelnen, geschützt das Recht des Einzelnen in dem der Gesamtheit; und magst du heute auch noch gezwungen sein die Freiheit karg abzuzirkeln, dem Sklaven nichts von ihr zu belassen und dem Römer sehr wenig, auf dass die Freiheit des Ganzen gewahrt bleibe, im Reich der Erkenntnis wird die Freiheit des Menschen unumschränkt bestehen, und sie wird es sein, auf der allesumfassend sich die Freiheit der Welt aufbauen wird. Denn das Reich der Erkenntnis, zu dem dein Staat erblühen wird, das Reich der wahren Wirklichkeit, wird nicht ein Reich der Volksmassen sein, ja nicht einmal ein Reich der Völker, sondern ein Reich der Menschengemeinschaft, getragen vom Menschen, der sich im Wissen befindet, getragen von der menschlichen Einzelseele, von ihrer Würde und von ihrer Freiheit, getragen von ihrer göttlichen Ebenbildhaftigkeit" (22).

Broch gives expression to his political ideals through Vergil in the great dialogue with Augustus which forms the human pivot of the book. Some critics have seen homosexual undertones in the quarrel, and doubtless subconscious elements play their part; indeed, anyone familiar with Broch's artistic method would not expect otherwise. Foiled pride plays its part, Augustus having counted on the dedication of the Aeneid to himself. However, on the surface at least, the quarrel revolves around differing concepts of the state. Augustus' idea of the state is fascistic. In Vergil's opposition we see an echo of Broch's concern for the legal protection of minorities in his political writings. Vergil's idea of the perfect state is quite different: "Der Wahrheit zu, in die Wahrheit hinein wächst der Staat, ihr gilt sein inneres Wachstum, in ihr findet er seine endgültige Wirklichkeit" (23). Here we come very close to what Broch meant by "the earthly absolute".

In the solitude of his darkened room, far from the thronging crowd, Vergil looks out on the sea, listening. His whole life had been spent listening, listening for death, as he now realises in the hyperclarity of fever, listening to the seed of death, which is our mortal inheritance, unfolding to growth. "Ein Wegsuchender im Gewölbe des Todes", Vergil had deserted the professions of doctor, astronomer, philosopher - all devoted to knowledge of life - for the pursuit of poetry, strangest of all human activities, the only one dedicated to the knowledge of death. He hoped in this way to grasp truth, knowledge, ultimate reality, for

der Tod ist erfüllt von all der Vielfalt, die aus der Einheit hervorgegangen

war, um sich in ihm wieder zur Einheit zu schliessen, er ist erfüllt von der
Herdenweisheit des Beginns und von der Vereinzelungserkenntnis des Endes,
sie beide zu einer einzigen Sekunde des Seins zusammenfassend, zu jener
Sekunde, die bereits die des Nicht-Seins ist, denn in unaufhörlichem Wechsel-
spiel mit dem Seinsablauf steht der Tod, und unablässig wird der in ihn einmün-
dende, von ihm empfangene und ursprungwärts rückgewandte Zeitenablauf zur
Einheit des Gedächtnisses verwandelt, zum Gedächtnis der Welten und Aber-
Welten, zum Gedächtnis des Gottes: nur wer den Tod auf sich nimmt, vermag
den Ring im Irdischen zu schliessen, nur wer des Todes Auge sucht, dem
bricht nicht das eigene, wenn es ins Nichts schauen soll, nur wer zum Tode
hinlauscht, der braucht nicht zu flüchten, der darf bleiben, denn seine Erinnerung wird zur Gleichzeitigkeitstiefe, und wer in die Erinnerung taucht, dem
erklingt der Harfenton jenes Augenblickes, in dem das Irdische sich zum un-
bekannt Unendlichen öffnen soll, ... (24).

The poet is in a sense comparable to the priest, mediating between the heights
and the depths, duty-bound to the service of death, marked out by his special knowledge from the mass of common humanity. In dedicating his poetry to the chthonic
muse Vergil was fulfilling the true purpose of poetry in a time of cultural decadence
and spiritual crisis, such as Vergil's age, or Broch's own. For the Vergil of our
novel is not merely the historical Roman poet, but rather a figure of mythical proportions, an archetype of the poet. In making the orphic descent he is fulfilling the
task of poetry, for the cognitive task of poetry is the extending of rational knowledge past the boundaries of the rational, a descent to the depths of the irrational.
As so often in his work Broch seems here close to the surrealists but in fact, of
course, his aims are quite different. For Vergil and for Broch poetry is a search
for Erkenntnis, a knowledge which aims at being total. This totality can only be
attained by exploring the nature of death, for

> "Totalität bedeutet nicht mehr die Enzyklopädik der sichtbaren Welt, son-
> dern das Universale und Vieldimensionale einer im mystisch-abstrahieren-
> den Erkennen bis ins Unendliche geweiterten inneren Welt, eines "diesseiti-
> gen Jenseits". Es wird erkennbar erst vom Tode aus, im Augenblick der vollen
> Einheit und Gegenwärtigkeit des bis in das Unbewusste hinein erinnerten Le-
> bens, und im Augenblick der imaginativen Vorwegnahme der Wiedergeburt
> zur mystischen Vereinigung mit dem Zeitlos-Einheitlichen. Denn alles Er-
> zählen Brochs ist ein Erzählen vom Tode und zum Tode hin, der sich als die
> Schwelle des hoffnungsvollen Uebergangs darstellt" (25).

In as much as poetry seeks knowledge of Being it strives, in Broch's mystical
concept, for knowledge of death and is at the same time a hope and a longing for
a reality beyond death. In death is fulfilled simultaneity, beyond time, space and
the categories of individuated existence.

Vergil inherited the legacy of Orpheus and dedicated his lays to the dark
muse, to that "truth sunk in depths of earth and gloom". He saw the transience and
frail mortality of man, the skull and skeleton behind the agitated and animated masks
in the bright Tändelmarkt of life. Having exposed the fragility and vulnerability of
the human condition, Vergil had offered mankind by way of spiritual consolation

and help nothing but the narcotic of aesthetic contemplation, the pseudo-religious worship of the aesthetic idol. Turning his back on suffering humanity he had enclosed himself in the narcissistic self-deification of creative solitude. Vergil's spiritual metanoia, to which I referred in the brief introduction, is largely a redirecting of the personality from this self-centred world of aestheticism to an other-directed love for "das Göttliche im anderen Menschen".

The aesthetic experience does not, of course, exorcise the ghost of thanatos but provides, as does eroticism, but a momentary release from the sphere of contingency. It cannot penetrate into the innermost spheres of reality, revealing ultimate truth, beyond time, beyond death, but remains this side of the epistemological boundary, earthly, merely symbolic, a mere game, a "Geschehen der Grenze", a mere simile, "Sinnbild der Zeitaufhebung, blosses Sinnbild der Todesaufhebung" (26), an earthly pseudo-infinity and therefore mere play.

As Vergil is carried through the streets on a stretcher he passes through a slum area. The people hurl insults at him, humiliating him. But this has a positive value: the destruction of his snobbery is a first stage of humility, the prerequisite of grace. Vergil accepts the people's scorn as being justified and sees his being brought to this place as not fortuitous. He accepts their scorn because his life has been empty, his work devoid of what alone justifies art-truth in the deepest sense. This explains the appearance of the three drunken and obscene figures: the connection with Vergil is that this pursuit of mere beauty in art is corrupt also. Through his sterile pursuit of mere beauty Vergil has made himself guilty of Meineid, the breaking of the contract between God and Man; he has betrayed the truth just as much as the staggering, drunken, mindless plebs in the gutter. We are presented in "Der Tod des Vergil" with a picture of a despicable mass betrayed by an intelligentsia composed of irresponsible aesthetes. There is an equal lack of proper values in all strata of society and rather than carry out his function of leader Vergil has failed like all the rest. He has not fulfilled his life's mission -- the resurrection of humanity.

Poetry merely beautifies the human condition, stimulates illusion, whereas mankind cries out for redemption from the tragic predicament. Like a narcotic poetry provides merely an illusion of release and redemption:

> nicht länger als der Gesang währet die Hilfe, währet das lauschende Innehalten, und es darf das Lied beileibe nicht zu lange erklingen, sollen die Ströme nicht schon vorher zu ihrem alten Bett sich heimstehlen .... soll nicht schon vorher der Mensch in seine altgewohnte Grausamkeit zurückstürzen, denn nicht nur, dass kein Rausch, also auch nicht der von der Schönheit erzeugte, lange vorhält, es ist überdies auch die Milde, der Mensch und Tier sich da gefangen gegeben haben, bloss die eine Hälfte des Schönheitsrausches, während die andere, nicht minder starke und zumeist sogar weitaus stärkere die der ärgsten Grausamkeitsübersteigerung ist -- gerade der Grausamste liebt es, sich an einer Blume zu entzücken --, so dass die Schönheit und gar die von der Kunst getragene Schönheit sehr bald ihre Wirkung verliert, wenn sie, des waaghaltenden Wechselspieles ihrer beiden Hälften nicht achtend, sich bloss mit einer von ihnen an den Menschen wenden will (27).

Even Orpheus, who could perform miracles with his gift of song, was subject to the limitations of the aesthetic, a provider of narcotic oblivion, and not of true redemption, of salvation from death. The true bringer of salvation -- and here we recall Broch's statement that Vergil was "one of those who are necessary that the prophet shall appear ..... a pre-prophet" -- has passed beyond the language of beauty, beyond the surface of that reality which poetry represents

> zu den schlichten Worten vorgedrungen, die kraft ihrer Todesnähe und Todeserkenntnis die Fähigkeit gewonnen haben, an die Versperrtheit des Nebenmenschen zu pochen, seine Angst und seine Grausamkeit zu beruhigen und ihn der echten Hilfe zugänglich zu machen, er ist vorgedrungen zu der schlichten Sprache unmittelbarer Güte, zur Sprache der unmittelbaren menschlichen Tugend, zur Sprache der Erweckung (28).

This language was what Orpheus was seeking when he descended into the shades in quest of Euridice. Orpheus, Vergil reflects, must have also felt the helpless despair of the artist, "ein Schreibender diesseits der Grenze, obwohl er den sibyl-lischen Auftrag entgegengenommen und fromm gleich Aeneas, eidleistend, der Priesterin hohen Altar berührt hat" (29). Vergil had tried to seize the nature of death in a web of images and similes, but the image is in itself not knowledge, with symbols and images one can merely circumscribe death, but not penetrate its ultimate reality. Like Orpheus or Aeneis one must pass the threshold of our space-time existence, dive down into the chthonic world of Pluto's realm. Yet Vergil will do this with a different aim in mind from that of his hero Aeneis:

> Aeneas ist dem Tod zu den Unterweltschatten nachgefolgt und ist mit leeren Händen zurückgekehrt, er selber ein leeres Gleichnis, ohne Heil, ohne Wahr-heit, ohne Wirklichkeitswahrheit, so dass sein Wagnis kaum weniger vergeb-lich gewesen war als das des unglückseligen Orpheus, obwohl er nicht wie dieser der Geliebten halber hinabgestiegen war, sondern um des gesetzes-stiftenden Ur-Ahns willen -; nein, die Kräfte hatten nicht ausgereicht zu noch tieferem Einstieg, und nun hiess es das Opfer vollziehen, nun hiess es selber mitsamt dem Gedicht das Nichts erreichen, auf dass die Todeswirk-lichkeit erstehe, sprengend das leere Gleichnis (30).

The Orphic myth in "Der Tod des Vergil" is interpreted as a descent into the depths of one's being, taking the subject beyond the Ego to the It, the chaotic, impersonal forces of cosmic being, the ever-creative void from which all comes and to which all returns, the timeless common primaeval ground of being. Beauty, although frequently mentioned as related in essence to Truth and Goodness, is, in fact, the antithesis of these; it is in the deepest sense a-moral. In the discussion with his friends on the burning of the Aeneid Lucius puts forward the theory that beauty, truth and reality are but one. The Keatsian equation of beauty and truth is rejected by Vergil and Broch, however. Beauty as such and art pursued for its own sake are beyond Good and Evil, a sphere apart from moral goodness, governed by autonomous aesthetic laws and hence not subject to moral judgement. Consequently beauty and moral turpitude are not mutually exclusive, bull-fighting, for example, finding extenuation in the formal, highly stylised beauty with which the barbarous spectacle is executed, or to choose an example from Vergil's own age: the gladiatorial contests, the martyrdom of Christians were legitimised by the same reference to the muses.

Beauty, as every aspect of life, should have reference to a central value-system, to human values. Art, if it is to be justified, is to manifest the Noumenal in matter, to serve the Platonic idea. Broch's view of art, as of life, is thoroughly Platonic:

> künstlerisches Sehen ist die Fähigkeit, in den Objekten deren "platonische Idee", das "Ding an sich", zu ahnen; künstlerisches Schaffen heisst, dieses Ahnen im Materialen manifestieren zu können (31).

The true artist stands in the service of knowledge, bringing consolation to common humanity with his insights into absolute truth. His is the superhuman task of descending into the underworld and bringing back revelation to the world of mortals, of penetrating beyond the barrier of finite experience and expressing the ineffable. For knowledge is

> Auftauchen aus dem Abgrund, ist demütiges Auftauchen aus demütigster Zerknirschung zu neuer Demut, ist Heimbringen der Wirklichkeit aus dem Nichts, in das sie gestürzt werden muss, um wiedergeboren zu werden: Erkenntnis, dunkelheitsgeborene Wiederkehr im Gleichnis, die Wiedergeburt der Wirklichkeit, gewandelt im Abgrund, dennoch unwandelbar sie selber (32).

The question is, however, whether such a task can be carried out in a time of cultural decadence. We have stressed constantly the parallel which Broch saw between Vergil's Italy and his own twentieth century Europe. Especially in the dialogue of Vergil and Augustus the similarity between their age and our own is clearly underlined, Broch expressing through Vergil his own doubts as to the justification of art, indeed the possibility of art in such a time of decadence. Vergil feels the panic caused by the valuative vacuum felt at any terminal epoch in history, in a time of religious decadence when church dogma no longer ties together individual elements into a coherent whole:

> das Gestaltlose, dem er zu entrinnen geglaubt hatte, war neuerdings über ihn gekommen, nicht als das Ununterscheidbare des Herdenanfangs, hingegen sehr unmittelbar, ja geradezu handgreiflich, als das Chaos der Vereinzelung und einer Auflösung, die durch kein Belauschen, durch kein Festhalten je wieder zur Einheit zu fügen war; das dämonische Chaos aller Einzelstimmen, aller Einzelerkenntnisse, aller Einzeldinge, gleichgültig ob sie der Gegenwart oder der Vergangenheit oder der Zukunft angehören, dieses Chaos drang jetzt auf ihn ein, diesem Chaos war er ausgeliefert, ja, dies war es gewesen, seitdem der brausend ununterscheidbare Lärm der Strasse sich zu einem Dickicht von Einzelstimmen zu verwandeln angehoben hatte (33).

This is a very interesting passage, illustrating as it does the unity of Broch's work, to which I referred in my introduction. It could indeed be said that Broch only wrote one novel and the similarity in mood and intellectual content between the above and many pages of "Die Schlafwandler" is startling. There are other points of comparison, notably the attitude of Pasenow and Augustus to the spiritual crisis of the times—both take refuge in traditional religion rather than look forward hopefully to some new revelation of absolute reality. "Der Tod des Vergil" is, in fact, the most successful attempt to express what he was trying to express in "Die Schlafwandler".

The Orphic myth is thus seen by Broch as a symbol of the epistemological process in general. Broch's view of art is quite clearly romantic. Classical art with its formalism is seen as inadequate, and it is indeed dissatisfaction with this inadequacy that drives Vergil to the Orphic descent, to embrace the Void. Formal, merely beautiful art only has reference to the here-and-now world of flux, of eternal Becoming, of eternal return, an Apollonian facade masking Dionysian reality. True art and true knowledge penetrate beyond this, breaking the circle of form to attain a reality beyond the reality of flux, time-space, of fate, finding "die Wirklichkeitswahrheit des Gesetzes" (34).

What is this "truth of reality" referred to above, a truth which stands above and beyond the eternal return of the flux of space-time reality? It is, in a word, love. Reality is love. Christian love or agape -- and Vergil has been termed a Pre-Christian largely by virtue of his anticipation of love for one's neighbour -- rests on the recognition of the Holy in one's fellow man. To show this is the true goal of art, surpassing all questions of sterile formalism and aestheticism. And ultimately this recognition depends on self-knowledge, on the Orphic descent into the depths of one's being, discovering the divine unity of Ego and cosmos, of subject and object, of I and Thou, of life and death, inextricably interwoven in the dialectical web of Being, to penetrate to the Divine

> im All, in der Welt, in der Seele des Nebenmenschen, vordringend zu jener letzten Gottesverborgenheit, die aufdeckungs- und erweckungsbereit allüberall und selbst noch in der verworfensten Seele da ist -- dies, die Aufdeckung des Göttlichen durch das selbsterkennende Wissen um die eigene Seele, das ist die menschliche Aufgabe der Kunst, ... (35).

Sexual love, mere gratification of the senses, is placed by Vergil on the same level as aesthetic pleasure, equated with narcotics, both occupying inferor levels in the path of self-realisation of Spirit, or the path to salvation, to express the same in Christian/mystical terms. Faced with the same tragic view of human destiny and history as Nietzsche, fully conscious of the complex of problems raised by the tragic philosopher, as frequent references in the collected works show, Broch courageously refused to succomb to the aesthetic fallacy of his predecessor, to the absurd affirmation of the Dionysian. Vergil's passing beyond this conception of love and art is a prior requisite of his attaining grace, based as it is on denying Will. In an interior monologue Vergil rejects the Dionysian (36).

If agape stands beyond death, as symbolised in the Crucifixion, being a reflection of divine love, eros is seen as intimately related to thanatos in Broch's mystic vision. Lovers are so caught up in the sweetness of the illusion with which the Will ensnares them to accomplish its aims that they do not see the mask of thanatos shadowed in their features. In the sweet game they fail to see the macabre fiddler who leads the dance. They do not know

> dass alles Hinliegen zur Liebe stets auch ein Hinliegen zum Tode ist; ..... (37).

In the visit to the Underworld in Vergil's Aeneid Aeneas kneels before the altar and prays to the goddess. The prophetess begins to answer him: "Seed of the Blood Divine, Man of Troy, Anchises' Son, the descent to Avernus is not hard. Throughout every night and every day black Pluto's door stands open. But to retrace the steps and escape back to upper airs, that is the task and that is the toil. Some few, sons of gods, have been given the power because either they were loved by Jupiter in fair favour or were exhalted by their own brilliant heroism above the world of men. Along the whole way stand clustering forests, and pitch-black Cocytus coils and slides all round" (38). To accomplish this return Aeneas must carry out various tasks. First of all he must find the golden bough, dedicated to Juno of the Lower World. Then the body of his friend must be decently laid in a tomb. He shall take black sheep as an offering for atonement. Only if these conditions are fulfilled will he find his way back to the living. Aeneas and the Trojans build a sky-high funeral pyre from spruce, oak and giant rowan trees, as a monument to Misenus, in accordance with the conditions laid down by the prophetess. The last rites and respects having been paid to the dead Misenus, Aeneas is shown the golden bough by a pair of doves belonging to his mother. "-, also vom Gott wie vom Schicksal berufen, gemeinsam ihr Wille, ist jenem die Grenze geöffnet, dem die Heiligkeit letzter Pflichterfüllung und Hilfeleistung zusteht" (39). reflects Vergil. As he lies dying, Vergil reflects bitterly how he has failed in his life to accomplish the Orphic descent and find the golden bough of knowledge which was granted to Aeneas. It is this bitterness which lies behind his anxiety to destroy his work, to transcend the limited vision of aesthetic experience.

He had been denied the grace of penetrating below the surface of existence, below the surface of language and art, because of his human guilt, his incapacity to truly experience agape, to take another human being's fate upon himself, to transcend the bounds of his Ego and find his way through to the Thou. The Orphic legend thus has further reference to Vergil's anticipation of Christian agape. The search for the golden bough of knowledge is ultimately a search for love, not that love is identical with absolute knowledge, but a reflection of that truth, and the key to the finding of it. It is this Vergil tries to convey to his friends who cannot understand his desire to destroy the Aeneid:

> Das Gesetz? es gibt nur ein Gesetz, das Gesetz des Herzens! die Wirklichkeit, die Wirklichkeit der Liebe (40)!

If this is behind his decision to destroy the Aeneid it is also finally the reason for his changing his mind. Underlying the intellectual content of the dialogue between Vergil and Augustus is the human element-jealousy. In an apparently highly abstract and intellectual argument childish undertones creep in, childish quarrels are revived. But underlying all this is their deep friendship. Vergil changes his mind when he realises the real reason for Augustus wanting the poem. Their friendship is supremely important to him, friendship being a type of love, and any human relationship based on love is more important than a work of art. He does not want to repeat the mistake he made in his relationship with Plotia when his aestheticism made him appreciate her beauty but fail to appreciate her as a person. Love assumes a primary importance, as in the other novels:

> - oh Heimkehr! oh Leidenentlösung im Leide, das Wunder der Unsterblichkeit!

oh, wir dürfen es berühren, wir dürfen, vielleicht nur für die Dauer eines Herzschlages, wunderempfangend das Herz, dennoch für ewig das Unerfasssliche ahnend erfassen, wenn unser Schicksal, einschliessend und umschlossen, das andere auf sich nimmt, grösser geworden und geweitet in der Hingabe, eingeflüchtet und selber das andere bergend, wenn mit dem Wunder des zweiten Ichs, das wir durch die Brände tragen, uns die zweite Kindschaft beschieden wird, gewandelt und dem Vater gehörend, Erkenntnis, erkennend und erkannt, Zufall, der zum Wunder geworden ist, da er alle Erkenntnis, alles Geschehen, alles Sein umfasst hat, Schicksalsüberwindung, noch nicht und doch schon, oh Wunder, oh so sehr wiedererwachte Musik des Innen und Aussen, geöffnetes Antlitz der Sphären, oh Liebe - (41).

Love is the beginning of spiritual awakening as it was for Hieck and the narrator in "Der Versucher" and Pasenow. To attain a real, vital meeting of the Thou is to transcend the Ego. Augustus cannot understand the wisdom Vergil tries to teach him because he must first overcome his egocentricity (42). It is to overcome Will, to pass beyond the bounds of the finitely Human, of the humanly knowable,

Denn den Schmerz blosser Brunst zu lindern, haben die Götter den Menschen mit der Liebe begnadet, und wem sie zuteil geworden, der sieht die Wirklichkeit; er ist nicht mehr blosser Gast im Raum des eigenen Bewusstseins, ... (43).

Vergil realises what an empty life he has lead-devoid of love. To love is to have an intimation of divine Being, for God is love and in his infinite love he created man in his own image, out of unity diversity, a diversity which carries with it the possibility of return to the origins, to that Ureinheit of Being, from Zweiheit to Einheit. Man is created in the image of God by virtue of his capacity to experience love. The bond of love between man and God is, as it were, an oath to be kept on pain of death, an oath which is perpetually renewed by each individual toward his fellow man, the breaking of which casts man out of divine community. For the exclusion from human community carries with it exclusion from divine community (44).

"Vishnu", the Buddha is reported to have said, "decay is inherent in all things compound". Death and decay are inherent in individuation, in the diversity of creation. Yet, for the philosophical idealist or the mystic, a re-gaining of original unity is possible by discovering that divine centre of consciousness which is beyond time, space and death. It is this experience of the unity of ego and cosmos which characterises the later Broch works. Man qua "compound thing" is doomed to death. Yet the mystics have always believed that by annihilating the Self in its compoundness - its wishes, desires, thoughts - true purity of heart may be attained, the state of grace which enables one to pass beyond death and see God. It is this dying-to-self which Vergil later undertakes. In their wisdom the Oriental mystics recognised several paths to salvation, of which that of solitary contemplation and dying-to-self is but one. They considered that one may also find salvation in the path through the world by selfless devotion to others and by true caritas. For in crossing the bridge to another human being, in truly loving, one similarly transcends the bounds of the Self in its compound, space-time, mortal existence.

In the deepest sense love overcomes death, the most profound symbol of which is the Crucifixion. Death belongs to the Chaotic, the ever-threatening Void, that which is outside necessity, logical order, the noumenal logos, it is part of the chaotic contingency of Becoming, of space and time:

> allein im Zufall enthüllt sich uns der Tod, wir aber, uns selber nicht einschliessend, von uns selber nicht eingeschlossen, den Tod in uns tragend, werden von ihm nur begleitet, er steht als Zufall neben uns (45).

As we, failing to take our fate upon ourselves, are mortal, so our neighbour is mortal whose fate we have not taken upon ourselves, to whom we have denied our help,

> der ungeliebte Mensch, den wir nicht in uns einschliessen und den wir damit unfähig gemacht haben uns mit seinem Sein einschliessend zu umfangen, oh, ungöttlich ist er uns, ungöttlich sind wir mit ihm, so sehr Zufall mit dem Zufall, dass wir kaum wissen, ob der, welcher als Lebender vor uns auftaucht, der an uns vorbeigeht, an uns vorbeitorkelt und um die nächste Ecke biegt, ob er, Schicksalsgeschöpf wie jeder, Schicksalsgeschöpf wie wir, nicht etwa schon längst gestorben oder auch noch nicht einmal geboren ist (46).

In this vision of a love transcending death Vergil anticipates Christ's advent. One of the reasons for his wishing to burn the Aeneid is that he has realised, through grace, that the "bringer of salvation" is not Augustus, a mortal man, however great, but will be the son of God. It is this he tries to explain to Caesar in the stormy dialogue in which Vergil and Augustus speak past each other, the one still unable to think beyond the political-military ethos of Rome, the other already on the threshold of a new truth transcending that limited concept, indeed transcending all earthly knowledge (47). The boy Lysanias, who represents the divine revelation afforded to Vergil, the voice from beyond the boundary, foresees the sublation of the Roman ethos of naked power, force and slavery by a higher, divine revelation of love and peace, incorporated in the incarnation of Spirit, in the coming of God-Man in the person of Christ (48).

It is the message of "blessed are the pure in heart, for they shall see God" which Lysanias brings to Vergil. As in Ilse Aichinger's "Spiegelgeschichte" the end is really the beginning:

> nur wer zu den Anfängen vordringt -- oh, Forschen ist Gottesgedächtnis -- erinnernd und aber-erinnernd des Vor-Anfangs Wurzelregion, dem wird mit dem Ende der Anfang, und er erinnert sich jeglicher Zukunft, verbürgt in Vergangenheitstiefe, nur wer das Verfliessende festhält, bezwingt im Verflossenen den Tod. Unbegrenzt ist der Abgrund des Einst und namenlos. Dem Tode dienen die Musen, dienen vestalinnengleich heiligstes Feuer behütend, das goldene Leuchten Apolls (49).

For Broch as for Aichinger the Christian wisdom of becoming as a little child is self-apparent:

> "nur wer nackt Ketten trägt, dem wird die schlichte Gesinnung demütiger Gnadenempfängnis, nur er weiss wieder zu weinen, ihm spart das Wunder sich auf, und so zum Kinde erniedrigt, sieht er als erster das Licht" (50).

Vergil asks Augustus to exercise compassion -- an essentially Christian attitude -- and sets an example by liberating his own slaves.

In the final pages of the novel, as the poet passes over into eternity, as the unity behind apparent diversity is revealed, the boy Lysanias is transformed into Plotia, who is transformed into an angel, beckoning Vergil to join her beyond death. As Vergil is on the very theshold of what we call death, and which is really the beginning of true life, he is granted a vision of the ultimate symbol of all -- transcending love -- the Madonna and Child (51).

In the final section, "Aether - die Heimkehr", Broch attempts to describe how Vergil gradually passes over the boundary of finite existence into infinity, how he passes over into death. As I have stated previously, the goal of all knowledge for Broch is the attaining of the identity of ego and cosmos, the recognition of the divine centre of the human personality and the "outside world". The process of dying is experienced as a gradual growing toward this union of essence by a losing, a decomposition of all that is non-essence in the ego and non-ego. The categories of subjective and objective seem to lose their meaning, the boundaries of ego and non-ego are slowly erased. The change which Vergil experiences is a

Verwandlung des Aussen ins Innen, ... die Einswerdung von Aussengesicht und Innengesicht ..... (52).

No longer can one distinguish between the observer and the observed, all is dissolved into pure relation. This unity of subject and object leads to a further dissolution of consciousness where the dying poet is given a glimpse into the pristine unity of all being, beyond time, beyond space, beyond differentiation:

es war ein Teilhaftigwerden, es war ein Teilhaben an der Ganzheit des zwiefach verspiegelten Seins, es war ein Einbezogenwerden in das unendliche Fluten der Gewässer, es war ein Durchdrungenwerden von der Innensicht der Unsichtbarkeit, zugleich aber auch das wissenlose Wissen an der Schliessungsstelle des Erkenntnisringes, des Nichts-Umfangenden, es war selber das Schliessen, es war der Zusammenschluss der zwiefach gerichteten Unbegrenztheit, in der die Zukunft zur Vergangenheit, die Vergangenheit zur Zukunft übergeht, so dass nun -- oh, Verdoppelung innerhalb der Verdoppelung, Spiegelung innerhalb der Spiegelung, Unsichtbarkeit innerhalb der Unsichtbarkeit -- es hier keines Mittlers und keines Gerätes mehr bedurfte, nicht des Bechers, der das Flüssige umschliesst, nicht der Hand, die den Becher reicht, kaum mehr des Mundes, der den Trank annimmt, es bedurfte dessen nicht mehr, weil alles Handeln, sei es Trinken oder was immer, mehr noch, weil alles Leben von der Kraft einer Verwobenheit aufgelockert und gelöst worden war, die jede Unstimmigkeit aufhob und keinerlei Teilung mehr duldete, ... (53).

Gradually time loses its duration. In the dusk of the sky and sea and the dusk of consciousness the soul seems to ebb and flow in unison with the tidal rhythms. Vergil enters a twilight state of consciousness in which all physical existence, all individuated existence in time, all particularity and contingency is dissolved in a higher level of being. A deep and lasting peace comes over all creation, that peace which passeth all understanding, the peace of infinity, of pure being.

die Unendlichkeit des wahren Lichtes und der wahrhaft schiedkräftigen Unterscheidung, welche die Gestalt nicht mehr aus Licht und Schatten, sondern ein-

zig aus ihrer innersten Wesenheit herausgeformt und erkennbar macht, so
dass auch hier Dunkelheit und Licht ineinanderflossen und oben wie unten
nichts sich finden liess, das nicht Stern und Schatten zugleich gewesen wäre;
selbst der Geist des Menschen, sterngeworden, warf keinen Sprachschatten
mehr. Ruhend war der Geist. Und Stern wie Schatten waren sie, die hier
wandelten; ihre Seelen gingen Hand in Hand, sprachbefreit; in sprachbefreit
keuscher Ruhe wurde ihnen Verständigung, und die Tiere, welche ihnen folg-
ten, nahmen daran teil. Ruhend wanderten sie, und dann ruhten sie von
ihrem Ruhen aus, Ruhen innerhalb der Ruhe, da es Abend wurde. Umlagert
von den Tieren ruhten sie und schauten hinauf zu der westwärts sich drehen-
den Kuppel, schauten hinauf zu dem stillstehenden Stern, ahnend in ihm das
Unsichtbare der zweiten Unendlichkeit hinter der Kuppel, schauten hinauf,
bis der Sonnenball sich wieder an die Dämmerung herabgesenkt hatte, und
ihr Schauen war wie ein Schauen von Schönheit -- freilich bereits jenseits
der Schönheit, denn bei aller Lieblichkeit, bei aller Leichte, bei aller
Tiefe, bei allem Ebenmass, es war das, was ihnen so mühelos zugestrahlt
wurde, keineswegs der Schönheit Nicht-Wissen, nein, es war Wissen, ent-
strahlt den innersten und äussersten Grenzen alles Seins, nicht etwa nur als
Sinnbild, nicht etwa nur als Sinnbild der Grenze, nein, es war des Seins
Wesenheit selber, dessen sie so mühelos teilhaftig wurden, dass nichts mehr
sich als fremd, dass alles sich als vertraut zeigte, jeder Punkt von Ferne
durchtränkt, jede Ferne zur Nähe verwandelt, und da wie dort alles zu ent-
rückter Unmittelbarkeit wurde, gemeinsam ihnen zuteil geworden, stiftend
die innere Verständigung ihrer Seelen (54).

In this insight into the innermost nature of total reality, this overflowing of the
bounds of self to attain an apprehension of total being, Vergil feels communion
with sky, star, shadow, animal and plant, feels himself flow into Plotia and
Plotia into him, feels his identity with all creation (55).

Thus, in the late works, Broch has come to a Christian, dualistic view-point
in which the fear of death and the fact of death are seen as only relating to man's
physical existence in time and space, in the here-and-now. The late works are
distinguished by a firm faith in the divine spark which is man's immortal heritage
and by virtue of which he can attain life everlasting. He who, like Vergil, has
sloughed off physical existence, who is living in and of the spirit, has overcome
death in himself (56). Death itself is seen not as the final extinction of a life
meaningless and tragic but as the threshold to true knowledge, true being, life
eternal. "In innerer Dialektik gebiert sich im Uebergang zum Tode als einem
Entwerden des Irdischen das höhere und wahrhaftigere Leben, das Erwachen aus
dem sehnsüchtig-dumpfen Schlafwandlertum im Irdischen, denn im Tode, der in
voller Reife der Bereitschaft übernommen wird, vollzieht sich der Schritt zur
Erkenntnis des Urgrundes" (57).

What of the novel qua novel? It is without doubt Broch's magnum opus, the
glorious fruit of his mature years, and, in the opinion of this writer at least, one
of the great novels of our time, a linguistic work of art to be placed alongside
Joyce's "Ulysses", yet lacking the spiritual negativeness of this other master-
piece. It was once described to me by a professional Germanist, who shall remain
nameless, as the most boring book he had ever tried to read (he admitted to not

having been able to pass beyond the first fifty pages). Such an opinion, I think, reflects more on its author than on Broch. Boring it is certainly not, except perhaps to those for whom literature means thrillers to while away the time on a train journey. It is, however, difficult and I think this difficulty derives partly from the extremely ambitious and daring nature of the task attempted and partly from the symbolic density and compactness which we have come to expect in a fine poem but not in a novel. In fact what the reader is faced with is a five hundred page poem - - a rather daunting proposition. One gains valuable and fascinating insight into this density of texture from a letter Broch wrote to Albert Kohn on the 7th of July, 1950 (58), which contains what is virtually an explication de texte of page 72 of the novel. Other great novels have passages of marvelous writing, of course, but one wonders how many of them would stand up to such close criti- cal scrutiny of pages chosen at random. Such a critical method -- de rigeur with poetry -- is not usually applied to novels and I cannot help thinking that if it were quite a few reputations would be destroyed. This demands, of course, great sen- sitivity and concentration on the part of the reader and one is tempted to level at Broch the charge which he levelled at Joyce -- that of obscurity. I personally feel, however, that whereas much of the obscurity in "Ulysses" is avoidable and defeats the object of a work of art, which is communication, the difficulty of "Der Tod des Vergil" is inherent in the theme.

Structurally it is Broch's finest novel. The intellectual content is fully assi- milated into the novelistic texture in a way not realised in earlier novels, particu- larly "Die Schlafwandler". As the novel opens we find Vergil approaching Brindisi harbour in a ship belonging to the imperial fleet. For the first time we are acquainted with the ship as a symbol of death. This central symbol gives unity to the symbolic structure of the novel. All the main themes are stated briefly in the first twenty pages of the novel, rather as in an overture, to be more fully developed later on. For example the thorny problem of art, one which was central to Broch's life and work, as became clear in the preceding chapter. The theme of democracy is introduced in Vergil's sympathy for the lot of the slaves (59). The platonic/ Christian philosophy of the whole work is indicated on page 18. The main theme of the problems of the modern mass, lacking any values and thrown into the void of uncertainty and doubt, is sketched on pages 21 and 22, some of the insights of the "Massenpsychologie" finding their way into "Vergil". The musical structure is further underlined by the division of the work into four major parts, correspond- ing to the movements of a symphony. To go more fully into the musical structure of the novel lies outside the scope of the present book, and in any case the per- ceptive reader will take great pleasure in discovering the structural subtleties of this symphonic novel for himself or herself. It is not, of course, the first time that such a musical structure has been used in the genre. Aldous Huxley's "Point Counterpoint" is another notable example but strikes one as contrived and preten- tious in comparison with Broch's work, too slick and merely intellectual and lacking in real artistic inspiration -- a symphony composed by a computer, as it were.

Stylistically the novel is perhaps unique in German literature, its linguistic and narrative innovations inviting comparison with Picasso's paintings and Stravinsky's music. Many passages give evidence of Broch's remarkable stream of consciousness technique:

Etwas Fürchterliches, das ihn von aussen und von innen zugleich anpackte, etwas grässlich Unbekanntes riss ihn hoch, jählings, aufschmetternd-bösartig, überschmerzlich-schmerzhaft, riss ihn hoch mit all der wüsten, lähmungssprengenden, erstickungsverzweifelten Kraft, die dem ersten Blitzdonner eines ausbrechenden Gewitters innewohnt, so fuhr es würgend in ihn hinein, todbringend, toddrohend, dennoch die Sekunden wieder aneinanderrückend und den Leerraum zwischen ihnen blitzartig mit jener Unfassbarkeit anreichernd, welche Leben heisst, und fast war es ihm, als blitzte in dem Blitz nochmals die Hoffnung auf, fast war es ihm, während er, gefügt unter die eherne Klammer, atemrasch, blickrasch emporgerissen wurde, als geschähe es, damit das Versäumte und Verlorene und Nichtfertiggestellte nun doch noch, vielleicht sogar nur in dem Nu des wiederaufgelebten Sekundenatems nachgeholt werden könne; Hoffnung oder Nichthoffnung, er wusste es nicht, schmerzbetäubt, schreckensbetäubt, lähmungsbetäubt, wusste er es nicht, aber er wusste, dass jede Sekunde neuaufgelebten Lebens sehr vonnöten und wichtig war, er wusste, dass er nur für dieses Lebensaufflammen, mochte es kurz oder lang währen, emporgejagt wurde, weggejagt vom Lager der Starrheit, er wusste, dass er der Unatembarkeit des starrumwandeten geschlossenen Raumes zu entrinnen hatte, dass er den Blick nochmals hinaussenden musste, abgewendet von sich, abgewendet von den Zonen des Ichs, abgewendet vom Oedfeld des Todes, dass er noch einmal, ein einziges Mal noch, vielleicht das letzte Mal, den All-Raum des Lebens würde umfassen müssen, oh, er musste noch einmal, ein einziges Mal die Sterne sehen, und steif vor dem Bett emporgerichtet, gehalten von der Klammerfaust, die seinen ganzen Körper durchgriff und doch von aussen umfing, bewegte er sich steifgliederig, marionettenhaft geleitet, drahtig -- eckig und unsicher -- stelzig zum Erkerfenster zurück, an dessen Wandung er erschöpft sich anlehnte, ein wenig abgeknickt wegen seiner Schwäche, trotzdem noch aufgerichtet, um mit zurückgezogenen Ellbogen und taktmässig tiefem Atem seinem Lufthunger Genüge zu tun, damit das Sein sich wieder öffne, teilnehmend am Atemfluten der wiederersehnten Sphären (60).

If the style of "Der Tod des Vergil" is highly remarkable there is no question of stylistic virtuosity for its own sake. Rather is the form -- as in any great work of art -- related to the content, in this case the two forming an indissoluble unity. This can be well illustrated by taking one feature of the style -- the interchangeability of images from one sphere to another. This reflects the basic theme of the unity of all creation. Broch is describing trans-sensual essences:

Noch wartete er, wartete, dass die Nacht sich nochmals melde, dass sie ihm Endgültiges und Tröstliches zuraune, dass sie mit ihrem Rieseln nochmals seine Sehnsucht wachriefe. Kaum war es noch Hoffnung zu nennen, eher Hoffnung auf die Hoffnung, kaum noch Flucht vor der Zeitlosigkeit, eher Flucht vor der Flucht. Es gab keine Zeit, keine Sehnsucht, keine Hoffnung mehr, weder für das Leben noch für das Sterben; es gab keine Nacht mehr. Es gab kaum ein Warten mehr, höchstens noch Ungeduld, welche Ungeduld erwartete. Er hielt die Hände verschränkt, und der Daumen der Linken rührte an den Stein des Ringes. So sass er, spürte an seinem Knie die Wärme der bis zur

Anlehnungsnähe herangerückten, dennoch nicht angelehnten Knabenschulter, und es verlangte ihn sehr, die verschränkten Finger aus ihrer zunehmenden Verkrampfung zu lösen, um unbemerkt-sachte über die nachtdunklen wirren, kindlichen Haare, auf die er hinabschaute, zu streichen, um das nächtlich Spriessende, nächtlich Menschliche des nachtweichen knisternden Flors durch die Finger gleiten zu lassen, nachtsehnsüchtig nach Sehnsucht; indes, er tat keine Bewegung, und schliesslich, obwohl es ihm schwerfiel, die Starrheit des Wartens zu unterbrechen, sagte er: "Es ist zu spät. " Der Knabe hob langsam das Gesicht zu ihm empor, so verständnisvoll und fragend, als wäre ihm etwas vorgelesen worden, dessen Fortsetzung nun folgen müsste, und dieser Frage gehorchend, sein eigenes Gesicht dem des Knaben sanft zugenähert, wiederholte er sehr leise: "es ist zu spät" (61).

Broch's style in "Vergil" sometimes comes close to surrealism:

das Zimmer schwebte mit ihm, unverändert und dabei fahrtartig verformt, zeiterstarrt und dabei fortwährend sich verändernd. Starr lösten sich die Amoretten aus dem Fries und verblieben trotzdem darin, aus Malerei und Tünche lösten sich Akanthusblätter, menschengesichtig geworden und den Stengel zur gekrampften Adlerkralle ausgewachsen, sie wehten neben dem Bette dahin, die Fänge schliessend und öffnend, als wollten sie deren Griff-stärke erproben, es wuchsen ihnen Bärte aus dem Blattgesicht und wurden wieder darein verschluckt, sie wehten dahin im Unbewegten, oftmals sich überschlagend, oftmals wie in einem Wirbel der Unbewegtheit sich drehend, es wurden ihrer mehr und mehr, weit mehr als die Wandmalerei hergab, mochte sich diese auch ständig erneuern, sie entflatterten der Malerei, sie entflatterten der nackten Wand, sie entflatterten dem Nirgendwo, aus-gespien von den kaltbrodelnden Vulkanen des Nichts, die überall aufbrachen, im Sichtbaren wie im Unsichtbaren, im Innen wie im Aussen, sie waren Vulkanlava, hauchiger Schutt des Vorentstehens und des Verfalles, mannig-faltiger und mannigfaltiger werdend, je mehr ihrer wurden, aus der Leer-heit entstandene und entstehende Formen, die sich ausserdem während ihres Dahingaukelns ineinander und auseinander verwandelten, ungestaltetes und ungestaltbares Zeug, Blattwehendes und Schmetterlingswehendes, vieles pfeilartig, vieles gabelschwänzig, vieles mit langen Peitschenschwänzen, vieles so durchsichtig, dass es bloss unsichtbar-stumm gleich schweigen-den Schreckensrufen umherflog, manches dagegen bloss harmlos und einem blöd-durchsichtigen Lächeln gleichend, das sonnenstäubchenhaft vervielfacht, mükkenhaft unbekümmert leer umherschwärmte, den Kandelaber in des Rau-mes Mitte umtanzte, an den erloschenen Kerzen nippte, ... (62).

Certainly it is clear from what Broch said of the composition of the novel, to which I referred earlier, that the method of writing had much in common with that adopted by the surrealists. There is a difference, however, between the automatic writing advocated and practised by the latter and the writing in "Der Tod des Vergil". It may be true that Broch wrote down automatically in a trance -- like state the long, litany -- like sentences as they came to him but we know from his diary and other sources how much craftsmanship, how much shaping and polishing went into the work before the final draft. Indeed, perfectionist as he was, Broch argued bitterly over publication deadlines with his friend and publisher Brody, maintaining that another year was needed to shape the whole into a consummate work of art. This conscious shaping, the intervention of reason, was anathema to the surrealists, part of whose programme was a rebellion against reason and common sense and all that these represent. Philosophically Broch and the surrealists are poles apart and the Austrian novelist never had any connexion with the French-based movement.

Fritz Martini appropriately entitles his study of modern German writers "Das Wagnis der Sprache" and indeed Broch, to whom he devotes a chapter, is one of the most daring innovators in recent German, if not European, literature. Wilhelm Grenzmann writes of "Der Tod des Vergil": "Das Werk steht stilgeschichtlich einsam in der deutschen Literatur da" (63). He forces the German language to the very limits in order to express the inexpressible:

> es war auch kaum die Einheit der Schönheit, nicht der verschimmernden Weltenschönheit Einheit, die sich damit auftat, nein, auch sie war es nicht, wohl aber die eines klingenden Flutens im Unerahnbaren, nachteinströmend, nachtausströmend, es war die eines unerinnerten Erinnerns an ein Stillehalten, in dem das Unvollendbare sich vollendet, verbunden zur Schöpfungssehnsucht letzter Ur-Einsamkeit im unaussprechbar Unerreichbaren, in einem unerahnbar neuen Gedächtnis von sehr grosser Reinheit und Keuschheit, und das, was sein Lauschen vernahm, war in dem sehnsüchtigen Fluten enthalten, stammte aus der äussersten Finsternis und klang zugleich in seinem innersten Ohre auf, in seinem innersten Herzen, in seiner innersten Seele, wortlos in ihm, wortlos um ihn, die heischende und zerknirschende still-grosse Gewalt verdoppelt raunenden Ur-Grundes, ihn haltend und ihn erfüllend, je tiefer er ihr lauschte, allein es war sehr bald auch kein Raunen und kein Flüstern mehr, sondern weit eher ein ungeheures Dröhnen, freilich eines, das durch so viele Schichten des Erlebens und Nicht-mehr-Erlebens und Noch-nicht-Erlebens, durch so viele Schichten der Erinnerung und der Unerinnerung, durch so viele Schichten der Finsternis herbeigetragen wurde, dass es nicht einmal Flüsterstärke erreichte, nein, es war kein Flüstern, nein, es war der Zusammenklang unzähliger Stimmen, ... (64).

At his best Broch reveals a unique gift for describing -- in as far as words will permit -- the ineffable. A passage such as that beginning on page 242 produces in the reader that frisson one experiences when hearing Beethoven's late quartets or Mozart's last symphonies, that feeling compounded of fear, ecstasy and awe, the elation of standing on the threshold of absolute reality. Yet the written word can only occasionally give an intimation of such reality, restricted as it is by its own nature as a medium. It is more properly the sphere of music. The last chapter of "Vergil" is a colossal literary achievement, but at the same time a failure, albeit a magnificent failure -- an attempt to express the inexpressible. In trying to do this Broch is forced to use paradoxes like "das wissenlose Wissen". I am sure many other examples will spring to the reader's mind. It becomes, in fact, in the course of the novel, a rather tiresome stylistic tic. Broch is, of course, fighting an uphill battle, using language to try to make it transcend itself, a paradox which has faced many a mystic before him, notably John of the Cross. It is the paradox of all literature, as Broch sees it:

oh, Ziel aller Dichtung, Augenaufschlag der Sprache, wenn sie über alle Mitteilung und über alles Beschreiben hinweg sich selbst aufhebt (65).

If the work is a magnificent failure one must accord to its author the respect due to someone who aims at the impossible. Such a failure is surely more admirable than the success of one whose sights are set much lower. Whatever the ultimate judgement on Broch's art is, one is bound to admit that he is successful by his own standards:

die Pflicht zur selbsterkennenden Wahrheitsfindung und Wahrheitsäusserung, dem Künstler zur Aufgabe gesetzt, damit die Seele, gewahr des grossen Gleichgewichts zwischen dem Ich und dem All, sich im All wiederfinde, damit sie das, was dem Ich durch die Selbsterkenntnis zugewachsen ist, wiedererkenne als Seins-Zuwachs im All, in der Welt, ja im Menschentum überhaupt, und wenn dieser doppelte Zuwachs auch immer nur sinnbildhaft sein kann, gebunden von vornehere in an die Sinnbildhaftigkeit des Schönen, an die Sinnbildhaftigkeit der schönen Grenze, wenn es also auch immer nur sinnbildhafte Erkenntnis bleibt, sie ist gerade infolge solcher Sinnbildhaftigkeit imstande, die unüberschreitbaren innersten und äussersten Grenzen des Seins trotzdem, zu neuen Wirklichkeiten auszudehnen, keineswegs bloss zu neuen Formen, nein, zu neuen Inhalten der Wirklichkeit, weil sich eben hierin das tiefste Wirklichkeitsgeheimnis, das Geheimnis der Entsprechung auftut, die gegenseitige Entsprechung von Ich-Wirklichkeit und Welt-Wirklichkeit, ... (66).

6. "DIE SCHULDLOSEN"

I propose to spend considerably less time on the final novel, for two main reasons. Firstly it has, in my view, formal defects which preclude it from inclusion in the great works, and secondly because the thematic material contains nothing substantially new, but rather a re-hash of ideas which are by now familiar.

As Broch was writing the later stories of "Die Schuldlosen" he was concurrently -- his letters bear witness to his extraordinary work-methods-writing his "political book", attempting to give a reasoned defence of the principles of democracy, and the ghost of the Nazi experience hangs over both works. Moreover, the political concerns of the theoretical book, as is usual with Broch, spill over into the creative work. The theme of the work has been aptly summarized by Hermann Kunisch as the lack of moral responsibility and moral commitment of the generation between the wars (1). The title poses the interesting moral theory that the technically innocent can, by their very lack of involvment, their a-social, a-political attitude to life, be guilty. The way in which the novel runs, at times, parallel to the Don Juan legend underlines the basic morality-play structure.

The novel was prompted by financial needs. "In 1949 Broch received the proofs of five early stories that his publisher wished to reprint as a book in order to profit from the succès d'estime that Broch had won with "The Death of Vergil". As Broch read through the stories, he became aware both of their insufficiencies and of the common theme that seemed to run through all of them. He decided to supplement the old stories with a few new ones, put them into a framework, and publish them as a "novel in eleven stories"" (2). These would hardly seem the ideal circumstances for producing a creative work which would sustain the level of "Vergil". Indeed the book suffers to my mind from a certain lack of concentration, born, no doubt, of working on "eight books" simultaneously -- and we know from the later letters what intense irritation diversion from his scientific work caused him -- in addition to his voluminous correspondence and various demands for academic work necessary to keep the proverbial wolf from the door. To my mind one can feel this lack of full attention and concentration in a letter of 16/5/49 to his publisher, Brody, who had requested the earlier stories for publication the previous year (I do not agree with Ziolkowski over the date here):

> Ich füge drei weitere Novellen ein, und das ist für mich leichter als Um-
> änderung (3).

It is as if the "Umänderung" is, quite simply, too much trouble. In a letter of 16/12/49 he expresses his irritation at being kept from his scientific work:

> Das Problem ist für mich umso ernster, als die Verschiebung der erkennt-
> nistheoretischen Arbeit mir eine ausgesprochene Qual ist. Zwei Romane,
> die einem wider den Strich gehen, ist ein bisschen viel für einen alternden
> Herrn (4).

In a letter to Hermann Weyl of 20/12/49 Broch indeed provides us with the appropriate metaphor for the method of approach adopted:

> Aber mir ist damals sozusagen aus heiterer Hölle ein Roman in den Schoss
> gefallen: ich hatte einem deutschen Verleger voreiligerweise die Erlaubnis
> gegeben, meine vor zwanzig Jahren verstreut publizierten, von mir längst
> vergessenen Kurzgeschichten zu sammeln und zu einem Band zu vereinigen,
> und als die Druckfahnen eintrafen, hatte ich das Gefühl einer Köchin, welche
> verdorbene Kost servieren soll: also tat ich das nämliche, was jede Köchin
> in einem solchen Fall tut: ich packte das Zeug in eine reichliche Beiz-Sauce
> ein (5).

To my mind the metaphor is both appropriate and highly significant, as is also
the adverb "voreiligerweise". In other words Broch was going to make the best
of a bad job, regretting his initial acceptance. In case it be objected that these
remarks are self-deprecatory I would point out that Broch always demonstrated
remarkable objectivity in judging his own creative work.

This is where I take issue with Ziolkowski, who finds that the novel "had
grown from humble beginnings to significant proportions" (6). As I see it the
work reflects all too clearly the tensions and frustrations resulting from the circumstances under which it was written, and can not be included with the major
works. According to Ziolkowski "Like 'The Sleepwalkers' it is archetectonically
structured, spanning the full gamut of styles from lyricism to essayism" (7).
One would wish that Professor Ziolkowski had not left matters there, with a bald
statement, but had treated us to a detailed analysis of this archetectural structure
such as his "Zur Entstehung und Struktur von Hermann Brochs 'Schlafwandler'"
(8). I would suggest that the mere fact of spanning the gamut of styles from lyricism
to essayism does not, in itself, constitute an archetectural structure. In a letter
to Rudolf Hartung of 2/1/50, replying to Hartung's criticism of the work, Broch
half concedes the shortcomings of the novel and gets right to the heart of the matter with his customary honesty:

> Ich hatte (und habe) den Eindruck, soweit man solche Dinge selber beurtei-
> len kann, dass mir die Darstellung dieser ungemeinen Komplexheit immer-
> hin gelungen ist. Nach Ihren Aeusserungen ist es mir nicht gelungen, und
> als Entschuldigung kann ich bloss sagen, dass es eben eine allzu kompli-
> zierte Aufgabe gewesen ist. Doch was lässt sich jetzt noch machen? Würde
> ich den ganzen Roman, wie ich es unter normalen Umständen jedenfalls ge-
> tan hätte, nochmals schreiben, so bin ich sicher, dass die Gestalt eine
> Plastizität gewonnen hätte, die dank ihrer Einwandfreiheit auch dem Leser
> plausibel geworden wäre; doch ich sehe nicht, wie sich das jetzt noch mit
> Flickreparaturen bewerkstelligen liesse (9).

I do not wish to labour the point, but here again I think the significant words are
"unter normalen Umständen".

Comparing the "Schuldlosen" with "Der Tod des Vergil" Hermann Weigand
notes a critical difference in the quality of organisation and formal discipline:
"Während aber das Sterben des Vergil als in vier klar herausgestellte Sätze einer
mächtigen Symphonie gegliedert erlebt wird, ist der Aufbau dieses Werkes von
verwirrender Kompliziertheit" (10). One cannot help but agree with this reaction,
even after repeated readings with the dedication and immersion in the work which

Weigand declares essential to penetrate the mysteries of what was to prove Broch's last testament. Weigand further remarks, quite rightly, that Broch deserves such dedicated and concentrated study. While sharing Weigand's profound admiration and respect for Broch the artist, I feel that this very respect has inhibited him unduly, preventing him from making an honest response to the work. I think the obvious point which emerges from Weigand's opening remarks in his introduction to "Die Schuldlosen" is that there is a basic failure of communication. I hardly need to emphasise the seriousness of this for while Broch repeatedly disassociated himself from commercial, popular literature -- Bahnhofslektüre, as he contemptuously described it -- his primary aim in turning from the fields of philosophy and mathematics to that of creative art was to communicate certain basic truths about life in our times.

Communication was of vital importance to him and no-one was more aware of the dangers of the esoteric than Broch, as the essay on Joyce amply testifies. My point, in brief, is that if a highly trained literary critic and connoisseur of Broch's works such as Prof. Weigand finds the work confusing, then how much more confusing it must be for the average educated reader. In terms of communication if one considers Prof. Weigand to be more or less an ideal "receiver" then the fault would seem to lie with the "sender". Nor does the problem, I feel, derive from the intellectual and imaginative effort required to grasp the complexity of the work, as is the case, say, with "Der Tod des Vergil". I once met a professor of German at London University who confessed himself unable to progress beyond the first chapter of the latter work and consequently dismissed Broch as "boring". The complexity of a great modern work of art would seem necessarily to limit the numbers of potential successful "receivers", except possibly in the field of music, where there are no cognitive or linguistic barriers to communication, although the possibility of subjective distortion still exists. A supreme musical genius such as Mozart seems to distill and resolve all the paradoxical complexity of life into one deceptively simple little theme in the slow movement of his piano concerto in D minor. It is perhapts Broch's tragic fate that due to the complexity of his art, mirroring the complexity of the reality it was its aim to seize, he has failed to have much significant influence in a world whose spiritual disease he so profoundly diagnosed, and so to communicate those truths which it was his life's mission to communicate, in the hope that the phoenix might rise again from the ashes. However, I do not feel that the difficulty of this work derives from its complexity, but rather from its formal defects, and also to a lesser extent from its surrealist tendencies, to which I shall later return.

Weigand's final remark is highly significant and illustrates his own ambivalent position: "Man war es dem Dichter schuldig, dem Geheimnis des Werkes selbst auf die Spur zu kommen. Ein Autor, der sich genötigt findet, das eigene Werk zu kommentieren, sinkt unter sein Niveau hinab" (11). With the advantage of having before us the letters published in the collected works since Weigand wrote these words we now know that this is precisely what Broch did, and, rather sadly, I must agree with Weigand's conclusion. To illustrate this point -- and also to elucidate some of the difficulties of interpretation -- I shall quote from some of these letters. In a letter to Frau Brody of 15/11/49 Broch writes

Und ebendarum ist es Ihnen auch nicht aufgefallen, dass die Zerline ihr altes Thema "Komm auf mein Schloss mit mir" wiederaufgenommen hat, also der Don Juna dem Juan recht nahe steht, und die Baronin nicht umsonst Elvira heisst. Und schliesslich der steinerne Gast.
Was aber den Imker anlangt, so ist er am Ende eben dieser steinerne Gast, dabei durchaus im Mozartschen Sinn ein ernster Bote des Himmels. Nun aber gehört es zu meiner Ehrlichkeit -- und nebenbei zu jener, die man vom Kunstwerk zu fordern hat --, dass ich nichts Unbewiesenes hinschreibe: wenn ich von einer Person behaupte, dass sie ein grosser Dichter ist, so muss das (wie eben beim Vergil) auch tatsächlich gezeigt werden, und wenn einer ein Himmelsbote sein und ausserdem singen soll, so darf beides nicht in der Luft hängen bleiben; das ist der Sinn der Benennung "Cantos", welche -- den Rahmen des Buches fast sprengend -- letztlich den abstrakten Himmel zeigen, atheistisch, wenn man will, dennoch eine _mögliche_ neue Form der Gläubigkeit; natürlich behaupte ich nicht, dass der Imker meine Cantos-Texte gesungen hat, wohl aber ist anzunehmen-- das ist einer meiner technischen Tricks --, dass das der Geist seines Gesanges war (12).

Now while the alert reader cannot fail to notice that the structure of the novel, such as it is, is loosely based on the Don Juan legend, the remarks in the second paragraph on the relationship of the Cantos to the Imker provide, I would suggest, an indispensible key to an understanding of this part of the novel and illustrate fully the point made above. A work of art should be self-contained and not require commentary from outside to explain it. I have, it is true, made liberal use of Broch's comments on his own works throughout this text, but in order to deepen and enrich our understanding of them. There is a basic difference, it seems to me, between this function, which I would suggest is the function of all literary criticism, and the commentary without which the work of art is incomprehensible.

Again, in a letter to his publisher, Brody, of 6/12/49 we find Broch having to explain some of the more obscure symbolism:

Steinerner Gast. Ich musste dem idiotischen Handtäschchen aus der "Leichten Enttäuschung" eine haltbare Symboldeutung geben, und da in der "Schwachen Brise" das Selbstmordmotiv angeschlagen ist, habe ich die beiden kombiniert. An irgend einer Stelle mussten die Schwächen der sonderbaren Herstellungsart dieses Buches zum Vorschein kommen. Und ich habe das umsomehr auf mich genommen, als ich das Uebernatürliche -- prinzipiell -- immer nur ins innere Geschehen verlege (selbst im Vergil), während es von aussen besehen völlig natürlich zugehen muss. Ein äusserer Sterbegrund für den A. hätte also auf jeden Fall gefunden werden müssen, und da war mir der Selbstmord immerhin plausibler als eine Prostataoperation (13).

And again in a letter to Rudolf Hartung from which I have already quoted a section:

Laut "Heimkehr" ist A. holländischer Edelsteinhändler, ist von einer gewissen, sehr schwachen Abenteuerlust besessen, sogar darin ein wenig zudringlich, wenn er auch ein gewisses Feingefühl für das Atmosphärische und die ihm begegnenden Dinge besitzt. Letzteres zeigt sich auch in der "Leichten Enttäuschung"; die Neugier steigert sich hier einerseits zur Lüsternheit,

sinkt aber dabei ins Weichliche herab, wird geradezu verschwimmend.
Abenteuerlust und Weichlichkeit, zwei disparate Dinge, und es hiess, the
best of it zu machen (14).

Here, more clearly than anywhere else, although the same can be read between the
lines of other letters, as I have indicated above, Broch acknowledges his failure
to weld together the stories with their often disparate elements into an artistic
whole. The letter continues

Ich habe mir mit dem Geldinstinkt geholfen; das ist A. s wirkliche Aktions-
fähigkeit, und weil sie ein wirklicher Instinkt ist, fällt sie ihm, trotz seiner
sonstigen Trägheit, nicht schwer. In diesem Sinn habe ich die "Schwache
Brise", die sein Jugendbild liefert, ausgebaut. Sein eigentliches Problem ist
seine Asozialität; sie entsteht aus seiner Trägheit und seiner ausschliess-
lichen Befassung mit dem Geld, d.h. beides macht ihn politisch "neutral".
Und diese Asozialität, gepaart mit seiner Lüsternheit, macht ihn zum "Ge-
nussmenschen". Sein Vater hat seine Trägheit ganz richtig erkannt, und aus
solchem "Erkanntwerden" entsteht die Prüfungsangst des Sohnes. Das Gegen-
gewicht ist die Mutter, um derentwillen die Trägheit überwunden wird; er
macht noch mehr Geld als der Vater, muss aber dann eine Ersatzmutter
suchen, für die das erworbene Geld tatsächlich verwendet werden kann; auch
diese Motive sind jetzt bereits in der "Schwachen Brise" angeschlagen. Von
der Mutter her stammt auch (psychoanalytisch gesprochen) sein zwiespälti-
ges Verhältnis zu den Frauen; seine Lüsternheit ist etwas Verbotenes, und
eigentlich schwingt in alldem der Wunsch nach Impotenz mit. Dies scheint
gleichfalls in der "Schwachen Brise" auf. Und der Weg vom Wunsch nach
Impotenz zu dem nach Selbstmord ist nicht weit. Hier aber geht die psychologische Konstruktion (und Struktur) in die metaphysische über. A. ist fein-
fühlig und intelligent genug, um seinen Selbstmordwunsch ins Fruchtbare
zu verwandeln und so löst er nicht nur sich selber, sondern auch die sicht-
bare Weltoberfläche, die Alltagswelt ins Nicht-Seiende auf. Er wird damit
zum Exponenten des modernen Geistes (15).

The abrupt transitions indicated above go more than a little way toward explaining
Hartung's difficulty in interpreting the text, and, I freely admit, my own, unaided,
that is, by Broch's commentary. And finally, from a letter to Karl August Horst
of 11/4/51:

Nichtsdestoweniger mussten die nun schon einmal gedruckten Stücke irgendwie gerettet werden. Und das konnte bloss geschehen, wenn etwas wirklich
Neues hinzutrat, um sie allesamt in sich aufzunehmen. Da fiel mir auf, dass
die "Leichte Enttäuschung" ein allerdings höchst unzureichender Versuch zur
Gestaltung des Erlebnisses absoluter Leere gewesen ist. Das war der Ansatz-
punkt, und ich stellte daher diese Novelle in den Mittelpunkt des Buches, das
Vakuum, die leere Zeit als Zentrum eines Geschehenssystems. Und es ist
auch das moralische Zentrum, denn daraus ergibt sich der Agnostizismus
des Prophetengedichtes, das seinerseits wieder durch die "Parabel" des
Eingangs und die "Vorüberziehende Wolke" des Endes im Sinnzusammenhang
gehalten wird (16).

I have mentioned above that the difficulty of the work also derives to some extent from its quasi-surrealist nature. Weigand remarks on the nearness of "Die Schuldlosen" to surrealism: "Man fühlt sich entrückt in eine Sphäre über- wirklicher, zeitloser Vieldimensionalität". And he comments further that the action "bewegt sich . . . . . in einem magischen Raum, in dem die Welt der Wirk- lichkeit sich zu schemenhaftem Schattenspiel verflüchtigt" (17). The word "über- wirklich" is, of course, the literal equivalent of "surreal". Wilhelm Grenzmann, who discusses Broch's oeuvre under the heading of surrealism, says of this oeuvre: "In die mystischen Tiefen des Unbekannten und nur Erahnten hat sich auch Hermann Broch versenkt und mit seinem Werk Zeugnis abgelegt von der Be- deutung der Erlebnisse, die dort für ihn bereit waren. Der Dichter verband das Dasein eines überwachen Wissenschaftlers mit dem Halbbewusstsein eines Träu- mers" (18).

Broch himself speaks of the stories as being merely the making concrete of a single dream-situation which has haunted him all his life (19), which comment, bearing in mind the central importance of images from the unconscious and dream imagry in surrealism, seems to support this view. Another section of the letter to Karl August Horst already referred to indicates the subconscious source of the symbolism in "Die Schuldlosen":

Dazu möchte ich eine Geschichte erzählen: ich habe den "Vergil" während einer gewissen Zeit nicht für Veröffentlichung geschrieben, doch als ich ihn später zu einem richtigen Buch umgestaltete, hat die Trance der Arbeit - - eine richtige Trance -- nicht nachgelassen; dabei stellte sich heraus, dass eine kontrapunktische Knabengestalt eingefügt werden musste, und das ge- schah mit der Person des Lysanias. Hier in Yale erfuhr ich nun von meinem Kollegen Faber du Faur, dass dieser Lysanias bis ins kleinste Detail die Attribute des Knabengottes Telesphoros (aus dem Kreis des Aeskulap) trägt, einer für mich bis dahin völlig unbekannten Göttergestalt. Solche Dinge kann man bloss als Richtigkeitsbeweise hinnehmen.
Und nicht anders verhält es sich mit den Dreiecken. Für mich war und ist das Grundsymbol der "Schuldlosen" das Nichts-Erlebnis, die leere Zeit, das leere Auge und ebendarum der Allblick der Blindheit, und ich kann da- her all die Dreieckkonstellationen, die sich notwendig und unbewusst daraus ergeben haben, bloss als Beweis für die Richtigkeit der alten Dreiecksum- rahmung des Gottesauges anerkennen. Es sind eben archetypische Vor- gänge (20).

The comparison with "Der Tod des Vergil" is interesting, as is the reference to the theory of archetypes of consciousness of Broch's friend and colleague, Carl Gustav Jung, and of course the insight we are afforded into the origin of the symbolism in both works.

At this point, however, it might be à propos to remind ourselves of the essence of surrealism, which is "Automatisme psychique par lequel on se pro- pose d'exprimer, soit verbalement, soit par écrit, soit de toute autre manière, le fonctionnement réel de la pensée. Dictée de la pensée, en l'absence de tout contrôle exercé par la raison, en dehors de toute préoccupation esthétique ou morale" (21). I think this excellent definition of the aims of the surrealist movement helps us to see quite clearly how close in some respects, and yet basically how far away Broch ultimately is from the former movement. While, as we can clearly see from the above passage, he submitted to the "dictation of subconscious thought" and conceived the basic symbolism in this manner, far from showing an absence of control exercised by reason, aesthetic and moral considerations Broch's work, taken as a whole, shows a rarely paralleled formal sense, an archetechtonic ability which fashions the raw material provided by the subconscious into a rounded, balanced work of art, the meaning of which is, in a sense, its form. Indeed, as I indicated above in the previous chapter, Broch did not share the revolutionary philosophy of the surrealists and had therefore no reason to take such a programmatic stance and abandon all the traditional elements of a work of art. If "Die Schuldlosen" gives the impression of being a surrealist work it is, I would suggest, because the surrealist element -- the highly subjective symbolism dictated from the subconscious -- has not been, as it was in previous works, notably Vergil, successfully integrated into the rational, formal, aesthetic framework. I agree with Grenzmann in seeing Broch's work as a unique combination of poetic inspiration and logical, rational discipline, unique, that is, since that other great scientist/poet and thinker, Goethe. Yet, at the risk of repeating myself, it is precisely this balance which is lacking in the present work.

Now I should like to look at the various sections in some detail. In the first section of "Stimmen" one has the impression that the rather overt didacticism has not been successfully accommodated in the lyric idiom; indeed, it is the view of the author that didacticism and the lyric are basically incompatible. The central section of blank verse is wooden, clumsy and one is tempted to question whether it is verse at all, but rather the by now familiar cultural-historical arguments on the decline of the West arranged arbitrarily in verse form. Truly, cold food warmed up and served with a piquant sauce to mask its insipidity! Furthermore, these arguments are far from clear in this form -- indeed this was inevitable when one considers that the very lengthy "Zerfall der Werte" is being virtually condensed into a few lines of verse. The despair at this cultural decline can be expressed lyrically -- one thinks of Kafka, inevitably -- but not in this way. While one knows Broch's genuine anguish at the cultural decline of the times, it does not communicate itself here. The old problem of the assimilation of the intellectual content (22) rears its ugly head. The novel in the early poems shows great unevenness. One feels that this section has been written because some short stories had to be pieced together, somehow linked to form a novel; there is a total lack of inner necessity, spontaneous creation, inspiration.

Chapter three (Verlorener Sohn) is a strange mixture of directionless, flat, uninspired middle -- brow story -- telling and incomprehensible pretentiousness.

In contrast, "Ballade vom Imker" is Broch at his best.

"Die Erzählung der Magd Zerline" is designed to stand in contrapuntal relationship to the more high-flown sections of the work, and yet in spite of himself, as it were, Broch's natural narrative gifts prove stronger and the story is full of pathos and, despite the crudity and grotesqueness, ultimately very moving. I feel this typifies the unevenness of the novel.

"Eine leichte Enttäuschung" demonstrates Broch's stylistic virtuosity. He uses a circumstantial, pedantically detailed, verbose and rather pompous style to describe, if that is the appropriate word, what is really non-action, or the very simple action of A. walking from the street into the building and slowly exploring it. The long time-duration of the narrative in contrast to the time actually taken by the action and the triviality of A!s observations create well the desired atmosphere of emptiness. The only real observations A. makes relate to the commercial exploitation of the rooms in the building, which is true to character, since his only real interest is money. A. is quite clearly a representative figure of the times. The style reminds one of Kafka, that other great chronicler of Western Man's spiritual vacuum, especially the Kafka of "Der Prozess", but lacks the salutory flashes of humour of Broch's fellow Austrian. Indeed, while conceding that Broch has attained his objective in this chapter, one is tempted to add the well-known appendage to the recognition of Victor Hugo's greatness: "Alas!."

In "Die vier Reden des Studienrats Zacharias" the novelists's hand is too apparent -- the meeting between A. and Zacharias is not at all prepared for. The purpose is obvious: to bring together these representative figures, alpha and omega, or rather A. and Z., illustrating between them the main traits in the population which allowed Hitler to assume power, which made the German people guilty, although technically schuldlos. The tone is different again in this story, this time satirically sharpened, even bitingly humourous, as when Z. asks A. if he is an antisemite: "hab's noch nicht ausprobiert" Andreas answers. Zacharias is a finely observed portrait of the petty-bourgeois, showing unquestioning obedience to the authorities and a completely closed mind. He is an anti-semite and rabidly nationalistic. I used the word "portrait" above, but of course Z. is a caricature, as indeed he has to be to serve the required representative function. Andreas and Zacharias-A. and Z. -- represent the two poles between which we are asked to accept that the German people at this time fell. Some readers may well feel that there is a certain crudity of judgement here, a certain over-simplification implicit in the method of caricature, illustrating the dangers of generalisation; yet there is, I feel, enough truth in the caricature to carry conviction, enough artistic vigour to make us suspend our disbelief, albeit temporarily -- Zacharias is a potent symbol, rather like the British Bulldog. A. shows his indifference to politics and yet the whole scene symbolises the unity of these two apparently different attitudes towards life. Whatever merits this story has as an independent unit -- and I think that merit is not inconsiderable -- it stands out like a sore thumb in the context of the novel as a whole. It is, as I mentioned earlier, not prepared for, it is extremely artificial and commits the cardinal error, on the part of a novelist, of not only manipulating the characters like marionettes, but being seen to manipulate them in this fashion. In short, it reveals the faults in construction of the novel and confuses the reader.

Even more confusing is the transition from the conventional story-telling of "Ballade von der Kupplerin" to the apparently surrealist style of the ensuing chapter. Indeed, this chapter is, in my view, incomprehensible without the author's explanation (see above) and fails to attain the artist's primary objective of communication. Also the style, reminiscent of Vergil, seems rather ludicrously inappropriate in the framework of this novel. One is reminded of Wagner's epigram quoted in Nietzsche's "Schopenhauer as Educator": "The German is awkward and uncouth when he wants to behave in a genteel manner; but he is divine and superior to all when he catches fire" (23)! Just such germanic extremes are exhibited in the work of Hermann Broch.

The penultimate story, "steinerner Gast", explains the book, in particular A.'s sin of indifference, and while it contains passages of undoubted merit which shine through intermittently like the sun behind clouds, by its very explanatory nature, full of sermonising, reveals the basic weakness of the work as a whole. The plot should carry its own burden of meaning, explanations should not be necessary, as Prof. Weigand pointed out in a passage quoted earlier, although interestingly enough he does not apply his own principle to his discussion of this story.

Indeed he describes it as one of the greatest achievements of Broch (24). Hermann Kunisch makes even greater claims for this central story in the novel. Making a comparison which is to a certain extent justified between the grandfather in the story under consideration and Mutter Gisson in the Bergroman, he comments: "In diesen Gestalten fand B.s Sehnsucht nach einem mythischen Stil, der in seiner archaischen Einfachheit und Abstraktheit dem Chaos der Zeit begegnen kann, seine halbe Erfüllung" (25). I can agree with this latter comment if one understands that the key word is "halb", although the comment represents an over-simplification of Broch's aims, as will shortly become apparent. Indeed, it is difficult to see how simplicity and abstractness, in themselves, can overcome chaos. There are, indeed, times when Broch seems on the threshold of breaking through to this new mythical style, but he never quite achieves it. In fact the whole work is a grandiose failure, much as "Der Tod des Vergil" was a failure, although on a lower level and for different reasons. If the "Vergil" failed it was because Broch therein attempted to express the Ineffable. "Die Schuldlosen" fails for much more mundane reasons:

Wegen des "Steinernen Gastes" habe ich soeben Dani geschrieben, und hier haben Sie's auch: kennen Sie das Verleger-Gehöhne gegen den armen Autor, der angeblich kein Manuskript aus der Hand zu geben vermag? Wehe aber, wenn -- wie es hier geschehen ist -- ein Manuskript zehn Minuten zu früh das Haus verlässt! Sofort wird gemerkt, dass da etwas an der Perfektion fehlt. Natürlich haben Sie recht: der "Steinerne Gast" hat noch schwache Stellen, und da bei meiner dichten Webung keine Flicken und Flecken anbringbar sind, gehörte das ganze Stück nochmals geschrieben. Doch diese vier Wochen darf ich mir nimmer leisten, und dies ist schade; der "Steinerne Gast" verdiente Perfektheit, gerade weil er auf so viel verschiedenen Ebenen spielt, hinauf bis zu einer, die beinahe in Vergilscher Sphäre liegt, hinab bis zu der des Satyrspiels, worunter ich -- Dani hat danach gefragt -- die Besitzergreifung des Ganzen durch Zerline verstehe. Und natürlich schmerzt es mich, dass ich da nicht das Letzte habe herausholen können; aber es war ohnehin ein Wunder, dass ich die Sache in so kurzer Zeit immerhin zustande gebracht habe (26).

The final story, "vorüberziehende Wolke", seems somehow tagged on, as it were, and, in fact, quite superfluous. But I should not like to conclude on such a negative note, but rather to consider what is in many ways the most remarkable achievement in this book, what Broch refered to as his "agnostizistisches Prophetengedicht". I like to think of this remarkable poem as being Broch's last testament to our generation, a beacon to guide us in our struggle toward a new faith. That Broch thought highly of the poem is apparent from a letter to his publisher of 6/12/49, in which he also explains the nature and purpose of the mythical style evidenced in this and the "Steinerner Gast":

> Ich freue mich sehr, dass Dir mein agnostizistisches Prophetengedicht Eindruck gemacht hat. Wenn Du dieses mit dem Gerede im Steinernen Gast zusammenhältst, so findest Du, was ich von dem -- notwendigen -- Wiedererwachen der abendländischen Gläubigkeit halte und wie ich sie mir beiläufig vorstelle. Und damit stehe ich nicht allein. Zumindest finde ich das nämliche in Kafka, und eben darum nenne ich ihn einen mythischen Dichter; sehr gerne würde ich das einmal mit allen Belegen ausführen, um der idiotischen Kafka-Auslegung der Literaten ein Ende zu bereiten. Und ebenso gerne möchte ich einmal einen mythischen Gedichtzyklus in diesem Sinn fabrizieren; das würde über den Vergil hinausreichen und dichterisch sozusagen das Endziel dieses, d.h. meines Lebens bedeuten (27).

One can only deeply regret that Broch was not granted the time to write such a work. There remains this poem, which gives us a tantalysing glimpse of what might have been:

> Ich bin, und Ich bin nicht, da Ich bin ...
> Mein Antlitz ist Nicht-Antlitz, Meine Sprache Nicht-Sprache,
> Und dies wussten Meine Propheten ...
> Denn soferne Ich bin und soweit Ich für dich vorhanden bin,
> habe Ich den Nicht-Ort Meines Wesens in dich eingesenkt,
> das äusserste Aussen in dein innerstes Innen- ...
> die Helle deiner Dunkelheit, die Dunkelheit deiner Helle,
> unerhellbar, unverdunkelbar: hier ist Mein Nicht-Sein,
> nirgendwo anders (28).

I feel that it is important not to misconstrue Broch's witty reference to this poem as an agnostic prophet-poem: this paradoxical title is designed to mirror the paradoxicality of the poem. Yet the paradoxes on which this poem is based are not the paradoxes of an unbeliever but the paradoxes of the mystic who has to resort to metalogical statements in order to express what is by definition beyond the reach of Reason. It is a deeply moving statement of faith by a man who all his life, in every sphere of activity, fought to keep alive the divine spark in Man, and in a way summarizes his whole work and achievement. "da, wo dieses Nicht-Sein Gottes ist, ist Gott. Er ist in Broch. In seinem Werk und in seiner Person ist die Gottesferne der heutigen Menschen, ihre Gottesfinsternis, wie Wilhelm Kütemeyer vor Martin Buber die Konstellation der gegenwärtigen Unfrömmigkeit genannt hat, wie in einem Gegendruck der Verzweiflung und der Gewissheit überwunden" (29), as Felix Stössinger, most perceptive of Broch's critics, aptly comments.

NOTES

Preface

1) <u>Gesammelte Werke</u>, Rhein-Verlag, Zürich, 1954, vol 8, p. 321.
2) <u>Gesammelte Werke</u>, vol. 10, p. 330.
3) <u>Gesammelte Werke</u>, vol. 8, p. 85.
4) <u>Gesammelte Werke</u>, vol. 5, p. 5.

1. The early writings

1) <u>Gesammelte Werke</u>, vol. 10, p. 221.
2) <u>Gesammelte Werke</u>, vol. 10, p. 10.
3) <u>Introduction to Gesammelte Werke</u>, vol. 10, p. 10.
4) <u>Gesammelte Werke</u>, vol. 10, p. 230.
5) <u>Gesammelte Werke</u>, vol. 10, p. 234.
6) <u>Gesammelte Werke</u>, vol. 10, p. 242.
7) <u>Gesammelte Werke</u>, vol. 10, p. 252.
8) <u>Gesammelte Werke</u>, vol. 10, p. 257.
9) <u>Gesammelte Werke</u>, vol. 10, p. 259.
10) <u>Gesammelte Werke</u>, vol. 10, p. 260.
11) Ibid.

2. "Die Schlafwandler"

1) <u>Gesammelte Werke</u>, vol. 8, pp. 17-18.
2) <u>Columbia Essays on Modern Writers</u>, p. 12.
3) See letter to Dr. Brody, 29/I/31 (<u>Gesammelte Werke</u>, vol. 8, p. 45.)
4) <u>Gesammelte Werke</u>, vol. 2, p. 20.
5) <u>Gesammelte Werke</u>, vol. 2, p. 24.
6) <u>Gesammelte Werke</u>, vol. 2, p. 25.
7) "Hermann Broch" (Columbia Essays On Modern Writers No. 3), 1964, p. 13.
8) <u>Deutsche Literatur im 20. Jahrhundert</u>, Heidelberg 1961, p. 222.
9) Ibid.
10) Ibid.
11) <u>Gesammelte Werke</u>, vol. 2, p. 37.
12) <u>Gesammelte Werke</u>, vol. 2, p. 38.
13) <u>Gesammelte Werke</u>, vol. 2, p. 38.
14) <u>Gesammelte Werke</u>, vol. 2, p. 38.
15) <u>Gesammelte Werke</u>, vol. 2, p. 39.
16) <u>Gesammelte Werke</u>, vol. 2, p. 40.
17) <u>Gesammelte Werke</u>, vol. 2, p. 563.

18) Gesammelte Werke, vol. 2, p. 50.
19) Gesammelte Werke, vol. 7, p. 235.
20) Gesammelte Werke, vol. 7, p. 235.
21) Gesammelte Werke, vol. 8, p. 26.
22) Gesammelte Werke, vol. 8, p. 57.
23) Gesammelte Werke, vol. 2, p. 152.
24) Gesammelte Werke, vol. 8, p. 18.
25) Gesammelte Werke, vol. 8, p. 19.
26) Gesammelte Werke, vol. 8, pp. 47-48.
27) Gesammelte Werke, vol. 2, p. 231.
28) Gesammelte Werke, vol. 7, pp. 73-74.
29) Gesammelte Werke, vol. 7, p. 74.
30) Gesammelte Werke, vol. 8, p. 48.
31) Gesammelte Werke, vol. 2, p. 273.
32) Gesammelte Werke, vol. 2, pp. 317-318.
33) Gesammelte Werke, vol. 2, p. 340.
34) Gesammelte Werke, vol. 2, p. 339.
35) Gesammelte Werke, vol. 2, p. 364.
36) Gesammelte Werke, vol. 2, p. 365.
37) Gesammelte Werke, vol. 8, p. 26.
38) Gesammelte Werke, vol. 2, p. 376.
39) Gesammelte Werke, vol. 2, p. 397.
40) Gesammelte Werke, vol. 2, p. 450.
41) Gesammelte Werke, vol. 2, p. 685.
42) Gesammelte Werke, vol. 8, p. 26.
43) Gesammelte Werke, vol. 2, p. 649.
44) Gesammelte Werke, vol. 8, p. 18.
45) Gesammelte Werke, vol. 2, p. 674.
46) Gesammelte Werke, vol. 2, p. 667.
47) Gesammelte Werke, vol. 2, p. 665.
48) Gesammelte Werke, vol. 2, pp. 682-683.
49) Gesammelte Werke, vol. 2, p. 577.
50) Hermann Broch, Columbia University Press, 1964, p. 18.
51) Gesammelte Werke, vol. 2, p. 505.
52) Gesammelte Werke, vol. 8, p. 60.
53) Gesammelte Werke, vol. 8, pp. 60-61.
54) Gesammelte Werke, vol. 8, p. 45.
55) Gesammelte Werke, vol. 8, p. 53.

3. "Filsmann" and "Die Unbekannte Grösse"

1) Gesammelte Werke, vol. 8, pp. 68-69.
2) Gesammelte Werke, vol. 8, pp. 67-68.
3) Gesammelte Werke, vol. 8, p. 76.
4) Gesammelte Werke, vol. 10, p. 337.

5) Gesammelte Werke, vol. 10, p. 342.
6) Gesammelte Werke, vol. 10, p. 344.
7) Gesammelte Werke, vol. 8, pp. 78-79.
8) Gesammelte Werke, vol. 8, p. 80.
9) Gesammelte Werke, vol. 10, p. 349.
10) Gesammelte Werke, vol. 10, p. 351.
11) Gesammelte Werke, vol. 8, pp. 81-82.
12) Gesammelte Werke, vol. 10, p. 282.
13) Gesammelte Werke, vol. 8, p. 87.
14) Ziolkowski, op. cit., p. 23.
15) Gesammelte Werke, vol. 10, p. 168.
16) Gesammelte Werke, vol. 10, pp. 168-169.
17) Gesammelte Werke, vol. 10, p. 169.
18) Introduction to Gesammelte Werke, vol. 10, p. 16.
19) Gesammelte Werke, vol. 10, p. 39.
20) Gesammelte Werke, vol. 10, p. 53.
21) Gesammelte Werke, vol. 10, p. 57.
22) Gesammelte Werke, vol. 10, p. 151.
23) Gesammelte Werke, vol. 10, p. 170.
24) Gesammelte Werke, vol. 10, p. 161.
25) Gesammelte Werke, vol. 10, p. 161.
26) Gesammelte Werke, vol. 10, p. 154.
27) Gesammelte Werke, vol. 10, p. 123.
28) Gesammelte Werke, vol. 10, p. 180.
29) Gesammelte Werke, vol. 10, p. 171.
30) Gesammelte Werke, vol. 7, p. 86.
31) Gesammelte Werke, vol. 7, p. 86.
32) See letter to Willa Muir 25/11/33 in Gesammelte Werke, vol. 10, pp. 353-4.
33) Gesammelte Werke, vol. 10, p. 18.
34) Quoted by Schönwiese in Gesammelte Werke, vol. 10, p. 19.

4. "Der Versucher"

1) Gesammelte Werke, vol. 8, pp. 144-145.
2) Gesammelte Werke, vol. 4, p. 555.
3) Gesammelte Werke, vol. 8, p. 319.
4) Gesammelte Werke, vol. 8, p. 156.
5) Gesammelte Werke, vol. 8, p. 131.
6) Gesammelte Werke, vol. 8, p. 138.
7) Ibid., p. 147.
8) Ibid., p. 148.
9) Ibid., p. 151.
10) Ibid., p. 155.
11) Gesammelte Werke, vol. 6, p. 202.
12) Gesammelte Werke, vol. 6, p. 204.

13) Gesammelte Werke, vol. 6, p. 205.

14) Ibid., p. 210.

15) Ibid., p. 260.

16) "Massenpsychologie" (Gesammelte Werke, vol. 9), p. 46.

17) Gesammelte Werke, vol. 4, pp. 35-36.

18) Gesammelte Werke, vol. 9, p. 82.

19) Deutsche Literatur im Zwanzigsten Jahrhundert, Heidelberg 1961, vol. 2, p. 222 (Wolfgang Rothe Verlag)

20) Gesammelte Werke, vol. 4, p. 419.

21) Gesammelte Werke, vol. 9, p. 101.

22) Gesammelte Werke, vol. 4, p. 79.

23) Ibid., p. 61.

24) Gesammelte Werke, vol. 9, p. 103.

25) Gesammelte Werke, vol. 9, p. 191.

26) Gesammelte Werke, vol. 9, pp. 124-125.

27) Gesammelte Werke, vol. 9, p. 110.

28) Gesammelte Werke, vol. 4, p. 89.

29) Gesammelte Werke, vol. 9, pp. 137-138.

30) Gesammelte Werke, vol. 4, p. 406.

31) Gesammelte Werke, vol. 9, pp. 181-182.

32) Gesammelte Werke, vol. 4, p. 228.

33) Gesammelte Werke, vol. 4, p. 226.

34) Gesammelte Werke, vol. 9, p. 107.

35) Gesammelte Werke, vol. 9, p. 113.

36) In a letter to Dr. Brody (Gesammelte Werke vol. 8, p. 123) Broch speaks of the inadequate treatment of the rationality/irrationality polarity in the "Unbekannte Grösse", due to the impossibility of treating the theme adequately in so short a novel and of the artificial end which hardly disguises this; to a certain extent "Der Versucher" makes good this lack, a later and more successful attempt to handle the problem.

37) Gesammelte Werke, vol. 4, p. 7.

38) Gesammelte Werke, vol. 4, p. 8.

39) Felix Stössinger in Nachwort Des Herausgebers, Gesammelte Werke, vol. 4, p. 583.

40) Gesammelte Werke, vol. 4, p. 425.

41) Gesammelte Werke, vol. 4, p. 246.

42) Gesammelte Werke, vol. 4, p. 355.

43) Gesammelte Werke, vol. 8, p. 103.

44) Gesammelte Werke, vol. 4, p. 48.

45) Gesammelte Werke, vol. 4, pp. 48-49.

46) Gesammelte Werke, vol. 4, p. 581 (Nachwort Des Herausgebers).

47) Gesammelte Werke, vol. 4, p. 494.

48) Gesammelte Werke, vol. 10, p. 277.

49) "Broch geht von der Sonderstellung des Menschen in der Natur aus, die er durch das in ihm wirkende Absolute begründet." J. Strelka, Kafka, Musil, Broch und die Entwicklung des Modernen Romans, Wien 1959, p. 88.

50) Gesammelte Werke, vol. 9, p. 277.

51) Gesammelte Werke, vol. 4, p. 324.
52) Gesammelte Werke, vol. 4, p. 396.
53) Ibid., p. 73.
54) Gesammelte Werke, vol. 4, p. 359.
55) Ziolkowski, op. cit., p. 24.
56) Gesammelte Werke, vol. 8, pp. 255-256.
57) Gesammelte Werke, vol. 8, p. 325.
58) Ibid., p. 104.
59) Gesammelte Werke, vol. 4, pp. 201-202.
60) Gesammelte Werke, vol. 4, p. 9.
61) Gesammelte Werke, vol. 4, p. 196.
62) Gesammelte Werke, vol. 4, p. 57.
63) Gesammelte Werke, vol. 4, pp. 199-200.
64) Gesammelte Werke, vol. 4, p. 37.
65) Gesammelte Werke, vol. 4, p. 258.
66) Gesammelte Werke, vol. 4, p. 112.
67) Strelka, op. cit., p. 68.
68) Gesammelte Werke, vol. 8, p. 184.
69) Gesammelte Werke, vol. 6, pp. 249-250.
70) Gesammelte Werke, vol. 4, p. 545.

5. "Der Tod des Vergil"

1) Gesammelte Werke, vol. 8, p. 217.
2) Glover, Studies in Vergil (Cambridge University Press), p. 227.
3) Glover, op. cit., p. 228.
4) Gesammelte Werke, vol. 8, p. 217.
5) Ibid., p. 217.
6) W. F. Jackson writes of Vergil, "Before he died he asked his friends to burn
    the Aeneid" (preface to Vergil's Aeneid, Penguin Books, London 1956, p. 12.
7) Gesammelte Werke, vol. 8, p. 218.
8) Ibid., p. 212.
9) Ibid., p. 214.
10) Gesammelte Werke, vol. 6, p. 265.
11) Strelka, op. cit., p. 86.
12) Strelka, op. cit., p. 86.
13) Gesammelte Werke, vol. 3, p. 83.
14) Gesammelte Werke, vol. 3, p. 9.
15) Gesammelte Werke, vol. 3, p. 29.
16) Gesammelte Werke, vol. 3, pp. 36-37.
17) Gesammelte Werke, vol. 3, p. 44.
18) Gesammelte Werke, vol. 3, pp. 53-54.
19) Gesammelte Werke, vol. 3, p. 402.
20) Ibid., pp. 99-100.
21) Ibid., p. 296.

22) Ibid., p. 404.

23) Ibid., p. 408.

24) Ibid., p. 89.

25) F. Martini, Das Wagnis der Sprache (Stuttgart 1959), p. 419.

26) Gesammelte Werke, vol. 3, p. 133.

27) Gesammelte Werke, vol. 3, p. 149.

28) Gesammelte Werke, vol. 3, p. 150.

29) Ibid., p. 151.

30) Ibid., p. 359.

31) Gesammelte Werke, vol. 10, p. 242.

32) Gesammelte Werke, vol. 3, p. 390.

33) Ibid., p. 96.

34) Ibid., p. 275.

35) Ibid., p. 154.

36) Ibid., p. 165.

37) Ibid., p. 26.

38) Vergil, The Aeneid, trans. W. F. Jackson Knight (London 1956), p. 151.

39) Gesammelte Werke, vol. 3, p. 151.

40) Ibid., p. 272.

41) Ibid., p. 232.

42) Ibid., p. 338.

43) Ibid., p. 276.

44) Ibid., p. 152.

45) Ibid., pp. 230-231.

46) Ibid., p. 231.

47) Ibid., p. 419.

48) Ibid., p. 291.

49) Ibid., p. 294.

50) Ibid., p. 295.

51) Ibid., p. 531.

52) Ibid., p. 489.

53) Ibid., p. 493.

54) Ibid., pp. 511-512.

55) Ibid., pp. 512-513.

56) Gesammelte Werke, vol. 5, p. 338.

57) F. Martini, op. cit., p. 423.

58) Gesammelte Werke, vol. 8, pp. 397-8.

59) Gesammelte Werke, vol 3, p. 14.

60) Ibid., p. 103-104.

61) Ibid., p. 77.

62) Ibid., p. 182.

63) Deutsche Dichtung Der Gegenwart, Frankfurt/Main 1955, p. 358.

64) Gesammelte Werke, vol. 3, p. 196.

65) Ibid, p. 91.

66) Ibid., p. 153-4.

6. "Die Schuldlosen"

1) Kleines Handbuch der deutschen Gegenwartsliteratur, München 1969, p. 124.
2) Theodore Ziolkowski, "Hermann Broch", Columbia University Press, 1964, p. 40.
3) Gesammelte Werke, vol. 8, p. 344.
4) Ibid., p. 368.
5) Ibid., p. 368.
6) op. cit., p. 49.
7) op. cit., p. 40.
8) Deutsche Vierteljahrsschrift für Literaturwissenschaft und Geistesgeschichte, xxxviii, 40-69.
9) Gesammelte Werke, vol. 8, p. 372.
10) Introduction to "Die Schuldlosen", Gesammelte Werke, vol. 5, p. 6.
11) op. cit., p. 6.
12) Gesammelte Werke, vol. 8, p. 362.
13) Ibid., p. 365.
14) Ibid., p. 371.
15) Ibid., pp. 371-372.
16) Ibid., p. 418.
17) Gesammelte Werke, vol. 5, p. 5.
18) op. cit., p. 357.
19) Gesammelte Werke, vol. 8, p. 344.
20) Ibid., p. 419.
21) Marcel Raymond, De Baudelaire au Surréalisme, Paris 1952, p. 282.
22) See chapter one.
23) My translation, Gateway Books, Chicago 1965, p. 68.
24) Gesammelte Werke, vol. 5, p. 19.
25) op. cit., p. 125.
26) Gesammelte Werke, vol. 8, p. 410.
27) Ibid., p. 365.
28) Gesammelte Werke, vol. 5, pp. 301-302.
29) In Deutsche Literatur im 20. Jahrhundert, Wolfgang Rothe Verlag, Heidelberg 1961, p. 224.